GOD'S FINAL CALL

GOD'S FINAL CALL

HOW THE BOOK OF REVELATION PULLS BACK THE VEIL
ON CURRENT EVENTS AND OUR ULTIMATE FUTURE

MICHAEL YOUSSEF

FOREWORD BY R. ALBERT MOHLER JR.

TYNDALE
MOMENTUM®

A Tyndale nonfiction imprint

Visit Tyndale online at tyndale.com.

Visit Tyndale Momentum online at tyndalemomentum.com.

Tyndale, Tyndale's quill logo, *Tyndale Momentum*, and the Tyndale Momentum logo are registered trademarks of Tyndale House Ministries. Tyndale Momentum is a nonfiction imprint of Tyndale House Publishers, Carol Stream, Illinois.

God's Final Call: How the Book of Revelation Pulls Back the Veil on Current Events and Our Ultimate Future

Cover design by Ron C. Kaufmann

Published in association with Don Gates of the literary agency The Gates Group; www.the-gates-group.com.

The URLs in this book were verified prior to publication. The publisher is not responsible for content in the links, links that have expired, or websites that have changed ownership after that time.

For information about special discounts for bulk purchases, please contact Tyndale House Publishers at csresponse@tyndale.com, or call 1-855-277-9400.

Library of Congress Cataloging-in-Publication Data

A catalog record for this book is available from the Library of Congress.

ISBN 978-1-4964-8637-0

Printed in the United States of America

31	30	29	28	27	26	25
7	6	5	4	3	2	1

Contents

Foreword

Blessed is the one who reads aloud the words of this prophecy, and blessed are those who hear, and who keep what is written in it, for the time is near.

REVELATION 1:3, ESV

Christianity is often classified among the major religions of the world. That is what we would expect from an increasingly secular world that sees "religion" as just another category of human experience. But a quick look at the Bible will dispel such an understanding. Jesus Christ, God in human flesh, did not come to organize a religion; he came to establish his church. Our Lord makes that clear in Matthew 16:18, where he declares, "On this rock I will build my church, and the gates of hell shall not prevail against it" (ESV).

This crucial text is exceptionally clarifying. First, Jesus Christ established his church, those he would purchase with his own blood, and he described his redeemed people in the most personal terms—*my church*. Second, Jesus declared that his church is safeguarded against even the gates of hell. While this certainly means that Christ secures eternal life for his redeemed people, it also means that no power on earth can extinguish Christ's church.

At the same time, the Bible is acutely honest about the persecutions and trials that will come to God's people. This was true in the Old Testament with the experience of Israel, and it is true in the New Testament in the experience of the church. By the time we come to the opening chapters of the book of Revelation, overt persecution and cultural seduction are openly challenging Christ's church, as seen in the experiences of several congregations in Asia Minor.

In that light, the opening chapters of Revelation, in the form of letters to the congregations of seven churches, carry significant weight. Jesus addresses these particular churches through a vision given to the apostle John. These letters tell us much about the challenges faced by these first-century churches. What Jesus says to these congregations is often bracing, sometimes even shocking. He calls out sin among the people, even as he assures them of his love. He indicts these churches for their failures and calls them to repentance. The living Lord speaks to his living church, even as many in these congregations faced the very real prospect of persecution—or even death.

As Christians today, we desperately need to turn to these letters so we can understand our own times and the challenges our churches face. Though two thousand years have passed since these letters were first given to Christ's church, each is as relevant and timely as today's headlines, and they reflect the experiences of today's Christians. Given the cultural seductions of the current age, we desperately need to hear and heed Christ's words to these churches long ago.

They are addressed to us as much as they were addressed to those early congregations in Asia Minor.

I am very thankful that my dear friend Dr. Michael Youssef takes us directly into Christ's letters to the seven churches. Faithfully, he guides us through each letter and accomplishes two very important purposes as he walks us through the text. First, he describes what each letter meant in its original historical context. Second, he speaks directly to the message each letter brings to Christians in our own day and age. His insights are clear, helpful, and incredibly timely. We desperately need to take heed as Christ speaks to his church.

To know Michael Youssef is to know his love for Christ, his love for the church, his love for the gospel, and his love for the Holy Scriptures. All those loves come together in this powerful book. Prepare to be challenged, prepare to be instructed, and prepare to be faithful to Christ in this present age. As Dr. Youssef rightly warns in this timely book, neutrality is not an option. That's a good thing to keep in mind—all the time.

R. Albert Mohler Jr.
President, The Southern Baptist
Theological Seminary

AN URGENT MESSAGE FOR OUR TIME

Persecution is coming your way. You may not have experienced it yet, but if you seek to live for Jesus, you *will* be persecuted, sooner or later.

That's the promise and warning Paul made to Timothy: "Everyone who wants to live a godly life in Christ Jesus will be persecuted" (2 Timothy 3:12). Are you ready to face the hostility and opposition of the coming days?

For many Christians, the day of persecution is already here. The global watchdog organization Open Doors reported in 2024 that active, oppressive hostility against Christians is rising worldwide. Today more than 365 million Christians around the globe suffer intense persecution. That's one out of every seven Christians around the globe. One-fifth of all Christians in Africa and two-fifths of all Christians in Asia already suffer persecution.[1]

Christians in America don't face torture and death for their Christian witness—at least, not yet. But the forces of anti-Christian hatred are growing in strength and boldness, both in the United States and around the world.

Here are a few examples of officially sponsored religious persecution already taking place in America.

We all remember how federal and state governments invoked emergency powers and inflicted penalties (including costly fines) to shut down churches during the COVID-19 pandemic in 2020. At the same time, these government officials allowed protests, riots, and looting to go unchecked in cities across America. They also permitted liquor stores and marijuana dispensaries to remain open, but churches were deemed "nonessential."[2] Now that government officials have gotten a taste of these lockdown powers, we can expect similar actions in the future.

The FBI has investigated parents—including Christian parents—for speaking out on a variety of issues at school board meetings. These parents should be praised and applauded for being involved in their children's education. They want the schools to stop exposing their children to pornography in the school library and to stop indoctrinating their children in perverse sexual practices and "queer theory." But because these parents have spoken up, the federal government—on orders from the US attorney general—is criminally investigating them for "domestic terrorism."[3]

A Catholic charity, the Little Sisters of the Poor, spent nearly a decade battling the Commonwealth of Pennsylvania in court. Finally, on July 8, 2020, the United States Supreme Court ruled 7–2 that these Catholic nuns did *not* have to pay for abortion-inducing drugs. Despite the Supreme Court ruling, Pennsylvania is still pursuing the Little Sisters in federal courts at the time of this writing.[4]

Girls and young women are increasingly required to accept boys and men (so-called *trans women*) into their restrooms and changing rooms. Not only is the male invasion of women's single-sex spaces an attack on Christian morality, but it violates women's rights and human rights. These rules are being imposed on us by the secular-left education establishment, the media, and state and federal governments.[5]

In recent years, Christian business owners (including a baker in Colorado and a florist in Washington State) have been targeted by LGBTQ+ activists and their own state governments, attempting to put them out of business if they don't knuckle under to a godless agenda. Even after winning their cases in the Supreme Court, these Christian business owners continue to be besieged and harassed by activists bent on shutting them down.[6]

Fired for Christian Beliefs

And then there's the case of my friend Kelvin Cochran, who served as a fire chief in Shreveport, Louisiana, and Atlanta, Georgia. In 2009, President Obama appointed him US fire administrator, a post he held briefly before returning to his job in Atlanta. Five years later, despite his being a highly decorated and qualified firefighting expert, he was abruptly sacked as fire chief of Atlanta *solely because of his Christian beliefs.*

While leading a men's Bible study in his church, Kelvin wrote a book to help men live purposefully and obediently for God. The book dealt with all aspects of a man's life, and it included a brief section—just a few pages—on the biblical teaching that sex is for marriage between a man and a woman.

After clearing the book with the city's ethics office and being assured he wasn't violating any rules, he self-published the book in 2013 and gave copies to the mayor of Atlanta and a few Christian members of the city council. He also handed out free copies to anyone who asked.

But in November 2014, the city suspended Kelvin without pay for thirty days—then fired him in January 2015. Why? Because a city council member who identified as gay was offended by the book's Scripture-based teaching on morality and demanded that Kelvin be fired.

With the aid of the Alliance Defending Freedom, Kelvin defended his First Amendment rights in court. In October 2018, after three and a half years of litigation, the city finally agreed to compensate him for violating his civil rights.[7]

Though Kelvin Cochran ultimately won his case, it has become clear that systemic hostility toward Christians and biblical values is widespread—and it's increasing. Government officials are becoming bolder and more aggressive in trampling the religious freedom of Christians.

As hatred toward followers of Jesus increases, we will be forced to either take a stand for Christ or retreat into cowardice. We will be forced to either proclaim our love for Jesus or deny our Lord. We will be forced to renounce our love for this corrupt and dying world or seek its approval.

Neutrality is not an option. We will have to choose.

When that day comes, I believe that many people in the church will make a tragic decision. Many who now attend church, sing hymns, and take part in Christian fellowships will fall away when the fiery persecution of the church heats up. Many will choose the world instead of the Lord. As Jesus himself said, "When the Son of Man comes, will he find faith on the earth?" (Luke 18:8).

We need to consider the coming days soberly and search our hearts honestly, remembering that Jesus said, "Not everyone who says to me, 'Lord, Lord,' will enter the kingdom of heaven, but only the one who does the will of my Father who is in heaven" (Matthew 7:21).

That's why we need to understand the book of Revelation. That's why we especially need to understand the seven letters to seven churches found in Revelation 2–3. These letters offer words of both warning and encouragement to the persecuted first-century church—and to us today. They instruct us in how to live victoriously in times of peril and hostile opposition.

More than a Book of Predictions

One of the most common misconceptions about the book of Revelation is that it is primarily a book of predictions about the future. Well, it certainly is that. But foretelling the future is *not* the primary purpose of Revelation.

This amazing book was written to strengthen the faith of Christians in the first century—and in every century after. The essential theme of Revelation is *how to live faithfully for Jesus in the here and now.*

We may think our own age is too far removed from those distant days of the first century AD. Our fears and worries are nothing like those of Christians in the Roman Empire. After all, we live in a time of global nuclear terror, bioweapons, cyber warfare, and the rise of artificial intelligence. What do we have in common with a culture that didn't even have printing presses, much less the internet?

But in taking a closer look at these seven letters, we find they were written during a time of intense political and social upheaval—and thus they speak clearly to our own time of political and social upheaval. The seven churches of Revelation 2–3 were surrounded by a culture of hostility, false religion, and in-your-face immorality—very similar conditions to those that surround us today.

The four Gospels—Matthew, Mark, Luke, and John—contain the recorded words of Jesus that he spoke during his earthly ministry. Acts 1 records the words Jesus spoke just before he ascended into Heaven. But he wasn't finished speaking—he still had seven important messages to impart to his church. The seven letters to seven churches in Revelation are the Lord's last recorded call to his people until he returns to earth in power and glory to establish his Kingdom.

As we approach the brink of eternity, the words of Jesus in these seven letters fill us with strength to face the present moment, and the courage to step out into an uncertain future. These letters show us that the risen and glorified Jesus will have the ultimate victory over sin and Satan. They teach us that we have nothing to fear as long as we remain faithful to the Lord.

In Revelation 2–3, we hear one sentence repeated seven times, once in each of the seven letters: "Whoever has ears, let them hear what the Spirit says to the churches" (Revelation 2:7, 11, 17, 29; 3:6, 13, 22). As you read this book, my prayer is that you will truly have ears to hear what the Spirit is saying to *you*.

WARNINGS AND ENCOURAGEMENT FROM JESUS

Many years ago, I visited a friend who was the pastor of the historic St. Philip's Church in Charleston, South Carolina. The congregation was established in 1680, and the current building was constructed in 1836, making it one of the oldest continuously worshiping churches in America. Three signers of the Declaration of Independence are buried in the churchyard. The eighteenth-century English evangelists George Whitefield and John Wesley both preached from its pulpit.

As we toured the historic church, my friend pointed to an ornately carved antique chair and said, "Please, sit in this chair."

I sat and gripped the well-worn armrests.

He said, "You're sitting where John Wesley sat when he was tried by the bishops and found guilty of enthusiasm."

Imagine, John Wesley was found guilty of *enthusiasm*! It seems hard to believe, but *enthusiasm* was considered a bad thing in Wesley's day. The Church of England looked down on enthusiastic evangelicals like Wesley.

The accusation of enthusiasm meant fanaticism, preaching the gospel, praying for revival, saving souls, and expanding the Kingdom of God. The fact that Wesley was not only *accused* but also *found guilty* of enthusiasm should make us ask ourselves, "If we were accused of enthusiasm for Jesus, would there be enough evidence to convict us?"

Patrick Henry for the Defense

Many people don't realize that evangelical Christianity was once persecuted in America. The oppression came at the hands of the Church of England, the state church of the British king and Parliament.

Church of England ministers were paid in tobacco, corn, and livestock collected from the colonists by taxation. One historian observed that most of these ministers "were any thing else than ministers of the gospel of Christ. Many of them were lamentably immoral."[1]

In contrast to the wealthy taxpayer-supported church officials were a growing number of "unlicensed" or "dissenting" preachers, poor men who faithfully preached the Good

News of Jesus Christ. As these congregations grew, the corrupt church officials began to feel threatened. Many joined with their local sheriffs to have the unlicensed preachers arrested for "disturbing the peace."

On one occasion, a sheriff arrested three preachers—Lewis Craig, Joseph Craig, and Aaron Bledsoe—in Fredericksburg, Virginia. When word of the arrests reached a Virginia lawyer named Patrick Henry—the very same Patrick Henry who had ignited the American Revolution with the words, "Give me liberty, or give me death!"—he rode fifty miles on horseback to the Spotsylvania Courthouse.

At the trial, Henry listened to the indictment of the three men, which accused them of "preaching the gospel of the Son of God." Barely able to contain his outrage, he stood and addressed the court.

"May it please the court, what did I hear read?" Henry said. "That these men . . . are charged with what! . . . For preaching the gospel of the Son of God!"

Patrick Henry reminded the court that the first colonists had left England and settled "in these American wilds—for liberty—for civil and righteous liberty—for liberty of conscience . . . to worship God according to the Bible."

Again and again, Henry recited the outrageous charges: "For preaching the gospel of the Son of God."

As he spoke, the audience applauded—and the prosecuting attorney turned pale.

Finally, the judge had heard enough. "*Sheriff,*" he said, "*discharge those men.*"[2]

Some historians say that religious liberty in America began with Patrick Henry's defense of these three pastors for the "crime" of "preaching the gospel of the Son of God." Unfortunately, we are now entering a *new* era of peril for religious freedom, as the following cases clearly show.

1. Protect a Life, Go to Jail

After the Supreme Court overturned *Roe v. Wade* in the Dobbs decision, the US Department of Justice stepped up its prosecution of Christian pro-life sidewalk counselors who pray outside of abortion clinics. The government began adding a charge of "conspiracy to violate civil rights," which carries a maximum ten-year federal prison sentence. The purpose of this federal strategy was clearly to frighten and silence Christians.

In January 2023, a jury acquitted pro-life advocate Mark Houck of federal charges that could have sent him to federal prison for eleven years. In 2021, Houck and his twelve-year-old son were volunteering for a Forty Days for Life prayer vigil at an abortion clinic. According to trial testimony, Houck moved to prevent a clinic worker from verbally abusing his son, and the clinic worker claimed Houck shoved him.

When local prosecutors refused to charge Houck, the federal government sent more than a dozen cars with about two dozen officers with guns drawn. The early morning raid and arrest terrified Houck and his family.

During the trial in Pennsylvania, the judge asked federal

prosecutors if the law hadn't been "stretched a little thin here" in trying to send a man to prison for eleven years over a minor sidewalk incident. Though Houck was acquitted, the federal government has continued to use the "conspiracy to violate civil rights" charge to intimidate pro-life Christians.[3]

2. When Christian Love Is Equated with Hatred

The FBI and other federal agencies have partnered with an organization called the Southern Poverty Law Center.[4] The SPLC built its early reputation as a scrappy group of public interest lawyers who won cases against the Ku Klux Klan and Aryan Nations. Today, the SPLC is a well-funded activist organization that vilifies some evangelical Christian organizations by labeling them as "hate groups." Housed in lavish headquarters dubbed the "Poverty Palace," the SPLC has an endowment of more than half a billion dollars.[5]

The SPLC publishes a so-called Hate Map featuring groups it claims spread hatred against minorities (including LGBTQ+ "sexual minorities"). On its Hate Map (along with the KKK and a variety of neo-Nazi groups), the SPLC lists mainstream Christian organizations such as the Alliance Defending Freedom, the Family Research Council, the American College of Pediatricians, the Liberty Counsel, the Pacific Justice Institute, the American Family Association, D. James Kennedy Ministries, and the Ruth Institute.[6] These organizations promote Christian love and compassion for innocent children, gay people, and people with gender dysphoria, while upholding biblical morality, and with a passion for proclaiming the Good News of Jesus Christ. But to the SPLC, Christian love equals hate.

On August 15, 2012, a heavily armed man walked into the Family Research Council headquarters planning to kill everyone in the building. He shot a security guard, but during the struggle, the heroic guard disarmed him. The gunman later confessed that he had targeted the Family Research Council after finding them on the SPLC's Hate Map. Though the SPLC recklessly inspired this attack, its leaders remain unrepentant, and the federal government continues its partnership with the SPLC.[7]

3. They're Coming for Your Children

Another attack against Christians comes from the so-called transgender agenda, also called radical gender theory or radical queer theory. There has been no national vote or debate over imposing this radical secular-left agenda on Western society. It simply burst onto the scene, taking mainstream culture by surprise. Leftist academics, media pundits, and politicians have adopted this agenda and are imposing it on our children by the force of law.

As I write these words, far-left Illinois politicians are pushing House Bill 4876. If passed, it would allow the state to take children away from parents who refuse to permit experimental sex-change drugs and surgical procedures to be used on their kids. The state would perform breast removal, surgical removal of genitalia, chemical puberty blocks, and other life-altering procedures on *minor children*, based purely on a child's temporary gender confusion. The bill would also take minor girls from parents so they can have abortions without parental consent.

Loving Christian parents who refuse to let the state mutilate their children would be prosecuted for "child abuse." Parents could face up to fifteen years in prison plus fines of up to $25,000 for the "crime" of protecting their children from these experimental procedures. The bill would give queer activists power over children while giving legal immunity to doctors who perform these procedures on children.[8]

Similar legislation is quietly being passed in other states. For example, a California law signed by Governor Gavin Newsom in late 2023 gives the state the power to take children twelve and older out of the home without a court order—and without the parents' knowledge or consent. California parents could face the nightmare of having a child taken from the home to receive "gender reassignment" treatments—and they'd have no legal recourse.[9]

LGBTQ activists often chant, "We're here, we're queer, we're coming for your children." When a reporter asked an activist if that chant means what it says, the activist replied, "It's all just words."[10] But it's not just words. They are telling you what they are *already doing* through legislation. They really *are* coming for your children.

These three examples just scratch the surface of the coordinated attack on our right to practice our faith in Christ. And it is getting worse.

Entering the Era of the Book of Revelation

By now you may be saying, "I thought this was a book about Revelation—but all you've talked about so far are American history and current events. When are you going to get to Revelation?"

I'll make the connection right now.

Revelation was written during a time of intense persecution, and I wanted you to see that intense persecution is happening today as well—as it has in the Western world in times past. If you think you're safe from persecution because you live in the United States of America, the United Kingdom, or Europe, think again. Persecution is already happening in the West.

I believe we are entering the era of the book of Revelation, and persecution will only get worse from now on.

Revelation opens with these words: "The revelation from Jesus Christ, which God gave him to show his servants what must soon take place" (Revelation 1:1). A revelation is an unveiling, an uncovering, a full disclosure. The Greek word for revelation is *apokalypsis*, from which we get such English words as *apocalypse* (meaning an event of final and catastrophic destruction) or *apocalyptic* (meaning ominous or cataclysmic). But in Greek, *apokalypsis* simply means "unveiling."

Revelation pulls back the veil on our uncertain future and reveals coming events. Most important of all, Revelation unveils the true glory and splendor of Jesus, the God-Man who temporarily set aside his glory—though never his divinity—during his sojourn on Earth. He is God the Son, who coexisted with God the Father before time began.

The apostle John received this revelation from the Lord Jesus in the first century, but it has never been more relevant than it is now, in the twenty-first century. Because Revelation was written during a time of great persecution in the Roman world, it still speaks volumes to us in our post-Christian age.

People think of Revelation as a book about the future, but it is even more urgently a book about the present. To understand how Revelation affects our lives here and now, we must look to the past.

An Apostle in Exile

Three days before Passover in AD 70, the Roman army under Titus, the elder son of Emperor Vespasian, laid siege to the city of Jerusalem. His goal was to suppress the Jewish rebellion by any means necessary. After a five-month siege, which led to starvation and unspeakable horrors within Jerusalem's walls, the Romans destroyed the city and the Temple and slaughtered all the inhabitants. The destruction of Jerusalem and its Temple happened exactly as Jesus had predicted some forty years earlier (see Matthew 24:2 and Mark 13:2).

After Vespasian's death in AD 79, Titus became emperor of Rome. But just two years into his reign, in AD 81, Titus died of a mysterious illness, and his brother Domitian became emperor. Today, you can pass through the Arch of Titus on the Via Sacra in Rome, built by Domitian in honor of his brother's triumph over the Jews. Carved images on the arch depict the despoiling of Jerusalem.

Domitian revived the imperial cult, in which the emperor was worshiped as a god. He gave himself the title *Dominus et Deus* (Lord and God) and demanded that people burn incense before his statue in every Roman province. As the smoke of the incense ascended, the people would chant, "Our Lord and God!"

By the time of Domitian's reign, most of the apostles had likely been martyred. Herod had executed James in Jerusalem. Peter had been crucified in Rome, while Paul had probably been beheaded. According to tradition, Andrew was crucified in Greece, Thomas was killed in India by a spear, Nathanael was executed in Syria, and Philip was crucified in Hierapolis in Asia Minor. The others seem to have suffered similar fates. John may have been the only apostle still alive.

By this time, he was likely in his early nineties and continuing to serve as a leader of the church in Ephesus. If you visit the ruins of Ephesus today, your guide will probably take you to the place where (according to tradition) John lived, and where Mary the mother of Jesus stayed with him in accordance with Jesus' instructions from the cross (see John 19:26-27).

John had taken a stand against the cult of emperor worship. He warned believers in Jesus not to worship idols. Their only Lord and God was Jesus Christ. The Ephesian

Christians refused to worship the emperor, and they suffered the wrath of the oppressive Roman government.

The apostle John was a thorn in the side of Emperor Domitian. To silence him, the emperor sent him into exile on the island of Patmos.

Many people mistakenly picture Patmos as a barren unpopulated island. In reality, it was a thriving Roman colony with an army outpost, shops, homes, and pagan temples. John was free to go anyplace on the island, but he was not allowed to leave it. He remained in exile as long as Domitian was on the throne.

The Apostle John, Time Traveler

In Revelation 1:9, John tells his readers that he "was on the island of Patmos because of the word of God and the testimony of Jesus." In other words, John had been exiled to Patmos by the Roman government because of his bold witness for Christ. He goes on to describe the vision he had there, saying, "On the Lord's Day I was in the Spirit, and I heard behind me a loud voice like a trumpet" (Revelation 1:10).

What did John mean by "the Lord's Day"? Some suggest he meant that the vision came to him on a Sunday. After all, don't we call Sunday "the Lord's Day"? I've even heard preachers say, "If you aren't at church on the Lord's Day, God can't reveal a vision to you like he did for John."

But that's not what John meant. Sunday did not become known as "the Lord's Day" until centuries after John experienced this vision. Sunday was simply called the first day of the week.

I don't think there's any real mystery about what "the Lord's Day" means. Throughout Scripture, the Day of the Lord is the Day of Judgment. It's the day when Jesus will return to judge the living and the dead. Here are just a few passages among many from the Old and New Testaments that support this view:

> See, the day of the LORD is coming—a cruel day,
> with wrath and fierce anger—to make the land
> desolate and destroy the sinners within it.
> ISAIAH 13:9

> Multitudes, multitudes in the valley of decision! For
> the day of the LORD is near in the valley of decision.
> JOEL 3:14

> Hand this man over to Satan for the destruction of
> the flesh, so that his spirit may be saved on the day
> of the Lord.
> I CORINTHIANS 5:5

> The day of the Lord will come like a thief. The
> heavens will disappear with a roar; the elements will
> be destroyed by fire, and the earth and everything
> done in it will be laid bare.
> 2 PETER 3:10

John says that when he saw the Day of the Lord—when Jesus showed him a vision of the Day of Judgment—he was "in the Spirit." John was privileged to see the long-prophesied Day of the Lord with his own eyes.

In the final chapter of John's Gospel, there is a scene in which the risen Lord Jesus predicts that Peter will die a martyr's death. Peter points to John and says, "Lord, what about him?" (John 21:21).

Jesus replies, "If I want him to remain alive until I return, what is that to you? You must follow me" (John 21:22).

In Greek, the original language of John's Gospel, the Lord's words are even more emphatic than they sound in English. Jesus says, in effect, "Mind your own business, Peter. My will for John is not your concern."

John adds that the Lord's words—"If I want him to remain alive until I return"—caused a rumor to spread among the believers that John wouldn't die. This rumor was probably still circulating when John was in his nineties. It must have seemed like he was indestructible and would be writing and preaching until the Lord's return.

I believe that when Jesus said, "If I want him to remain alive until I return," he was dropping a hint that John truly *would* see the Second Coming, the Day of the Lord. He would see that day when he received the vision on Patmos. In other words, the book of Revelation is the fulfillment of the Lord's words in John 21:22.

What does John mean when he says, "I was in the Spirit"? I have given a lot of thought to those words. In fact, I could write an entire book on what "in the Spirit" means—and perhaps someday I will. But the essence of his meaning is this: John lived in reliance on the power of the Holy Spirit.

When Emperor Domitian sent John into exile on the island of Patmos, he was trying to punish him, to silence him, to get him out of the way, to show him who was boss. The emperor thought he had defeated John; but John was not defeated.

Though separated from his Christian friends, he could not be separated from the Lord Jesus Christ. Though cut off from the fellowship of his home church, he could not be cut off from the Holy Spirit. Though deprived of his freedom to preach the gospel, nothing could deprive him of the Father's love.

The full weight of the oppressive Roman government could not crush John's spirit, because he was filled with the Holy Spirit. He was yielded to the Holy Spirit. He was strengthened by the Holy Spirit. He was comforted by the Holy Spirit.

John's enemies banished him to a far-off island, but God turned this exile into a panoramic vision of eternal reality. Because John was "in the Spirit," he was yielded to the Holy Spirit and not to his circumstances. God transformed John's punishment into praise, his isolation into revelation.

Because John was "in the Spirit," God swept him into the future to behold the end of human history. John became a time traveler when he was transported to the Day of the Lord.

If you want to gain the full spiritual benefit from these seven letters in Revelation 2–3, I encourage you to follow John's example. Go to the Lord in prayer and tell him you want to be "in the Spirit." Ask the Holy Spirit to fill you, make you wise and receptive, and help you to apply everything the Lord wants to teach you.

A Complete Picture of Jesus

The entire Bible is about Jesus. The prophecies of the Old Testament give us a picture of Jesus that is hazy and indistinct, but which gradually comes into focus.

In the four Gospels, Matthew, Mark, Luke, and John, the truth about Jesus becomes crystal clear. He walks the earth, teaching and healing and raising the dead. He dies—and he rises again!

In Acts and the Epistles, people who knew Jesus (including Paul, who met the resurrected Lord on the road to Damascus) fill in many of the details about who Jesus is and all that he has done for us.

Finally, in Revelation, our vision of Jesus is completed in every dimension. We see him, not only as the promised Messiah—not only as the preaching, healing, crucified, risen, and ascended Son of God—but also as the King of kings and Lord of lords, the glorified and reigning Son of God, coming to judge the living and the dead. Now our image of Jesus is complete.

Not only does the book of Revelation complete the picture of Jesus, but it also completes the story of humanity. Genesis and Revelation serve as the bookends for all human history.

At the beginning of the Bible, Genesis tells us about the origin of the human race—our splendid creation and our tragic fall. At the end of the Bible, Revelation tells us how those who have been saved by faith in Jesus enter into eternal fellowship with God.

Revelation reveals that all of history has a purpose. Though the world seems out of control to us, God is still in ultimate control. He reigns and rules, and nothing happens anywhere in the world when he is not looking. Revelation is a continuous unveiling of the glorified Jesus and all he will do in the future of the human race.

The book of Revelation divides into four parts:

Part 1, chapters 1–3: Warnings and Encouragement for the Church

Part 2, chapters 4–17: Judgment against Sin Poured Out upon the Earth

Part 3, chapters 18–20: The Final Destruction of Satan and Evil

Part 4, chapters 21–22: The Coming New Heaven and New Earth

In this book, we will focus on just two chapters in Part 1: Revelation 2–3. These two chapters contain urgent messages of both warning and encouragement to seven first-century churches in Asia Minor (now known as the nation of Turkey).

Revelation opens with John's greeting, and then he describes the moment when Jesus appears to him, dressed in a robe bound by a golden sash, with hair as white as snow and eyes like blazing fire (Revelation 1:13-14). Jesus tells John to write on a scroll all that he sees and hears.

Then the glorified Jesus begins revealing what he thinks of his church. Jesus chooses seven churches in Asia Minor to represent all churches, in all places, at all times. Seven, of course, is the biblical number of completion, suggesting that these seven churches give us a complete picture of the church in every age.

On a map, the seven churches form an irregular circle. If you depart from the island of Patmos, where John experienced his vision from the Lord, the closest city is Ephesus. From Ephesus, you would travel north to Smyrna, then further north to Pergamum, then southeast to Thyatira, down to Sardis and Philadelphia, and finally down to Laodicea.

Why is it important to understand the historical background of these seven churches? Because these churches were going through a time of persecution much like the times we are entering. By understanding the cultural pressures of Roman-occupied Asia Minor in the first century, we can apply the lessons of these seven letters to our own trials today.

The Satanic Strategy

In the late first century, the Christian church across the Roman Empire was suffering the worst persecution imaginable. Emperor Nero launched a wave of intense persecution from AD 54 to 68. Then, from 81 to 96, Emperor Domitian started a second wave of persecution—a far more systematic, wide-ranging, and deadly reign of terror than Nero's. Where Nero was brutal and sadistic, rounding up many Christians in Rome and burning them alive as torches in his garden, Domitian's persecution stretched across the vast Roman Empire.

Domitian demanded that all people worship him as Lord and God. Those who refused became outcasts. They were verbally attacked and insulted by their neighbors. They were shunned and threatened. Their businesses were destroyed. They were reported to the Roman authorities, and many were executed. Imagine their fear for themselves and their children. The temptation to compromise must have been overwhelming.

In addition to the external threat from their neighbors

and the Roman government, the early Christians faced the internal threat of false teachers, false prophets, and the infiltration of immorality. Satan—much as he had gone after Jesus in the early days of his life on earth—was now trying to murder the infant church in its cradle.

I've heard people say, "Well, that was then, and this is now. Things are different today." No, the things that truly matter haven't changed. Human nature hasn't changed. The dynamics of church life haven't changed. Satan's strategy hasn't changed. He still seeks to destroy the church Jesus founded.

But Satan could not destroy the first-century church, and he will not destroy the twenty-first-century church. Even though he can't win, he can wreak havoc and devastation. All Satan needs is one or two undiscerning or unfaithful people in a church, and tragedy will follow. One of his favorite tactics is to use false teachers to deceive the faithful.

In these seven letters, we see evidence of Satan's handiwork again and again. We see him orchestrating visible conflicts and invisible strategies. And one thing that becomes clear in these letters is that Satan attacks the church from multiple directions.

Sometimes he attacks through physical persecution.

Sometimes he attacks through governments, laws, and courts.

Sometimes he attacks through false teachers and false preachers.

Sometimes he attacks through the sins of compromising Christians.

In every age, Satan has been a dangerous and implacable foe. And as the day approaches when he will be thrown into the Lake of Fire forever, his attacks on the church will grow increasingly more desperate.

Satan is intelligent, but he's not very creative. His strategies never change. He uses the same means and methods today that he used two thousand years ago. Even though by now we should know his strategies by heart, we never seem to learn from history. We get blindsided again and again in every generation.

Just look at what Satan is accomplishing in the church around the world today. In America and other Western countries, he has caused the love of many Christians to grow cold—both their love for Jesus and their love for one another. He has tricked many into loving the world, loving material things, and loving themselves more than they love Jesus.

In other parts of the world, Satan has used false religions and authoritarian governments to systematically hunt down, torture, and kill believers.

Elsewhere, Satan has seized control of the citadels of learning, assaulting the minds of children and young people, filling them with false ideologies and misinformation. Beginning with kindergarten and continuing all the way through the university experience, Satan has turned our education system into an indoctrination factory designed to turn young minds against the faith in which their parents have raised them.

In still other parts of our culture today, Satan has convinced people that love means the acceptance of immorality and the toleration of sin. He persuades believers to doubt God's Word and to view biblical morality as bigoted and irrelevant.

As we will soon see, Satan used these same tactics and strategies to confuse, weaken, and corrupt the church in the first century. That is why these seven letters have never been more relevant than they are today.

Faithful to Jesus Alone

What is the central theme of Jesus' messages to his church in these seven letters? That he wants his bride, the church, to be faithful to him alone. The theme of faithfulness to Jesus runs throughout each of the seven letters. Our Lord either affirms a congregation for their faithfulness to him or reproves a congregation for turning away from him.

This theme of faithfulness shines in three dazzling facets in the opening paragraph of Revelation, where John writes that these messages come directly "from Jesus Christ, who is the faithful witness, the firstborn from the dead, and the ruler of the kings of the earth" (Revelation 1:5).

Facet #1: Jesus wants his bride, the church, to look only to him, the faithful witness. We're *not* to look to psychology, or to political ideologies, or to clever marketing techniques, or to worldly philosophies. The church must look to Christ alone.

The exalted, glorified Jesus introduces himself as "the faithful witness." Everything he says is true. Rely on it. Bet your life on it. His witness is faithful and dependable.

Do you want to share your faith with others? Do you want to see lost souls come to Jesus for salvation? Then follow his example by being a faithful witness.

Jesus never faltered or evaded. He spoke the truth, boldly and faithfully. Even when the Pharisees tried to trap him, even when Pontius Pilate tried to get him to change his testimony, even when the terror and pain of the Cross loomed before him, he continued to be a faithful witness.

Facet #2: Jesus wants his bride, the church, to place its eternal hope in him, because he is the firstborn from the dead. In the Gospels, Jesus raises three people from the dead: a synagogue leader's daughter (Matthew 9:18-26); a widow's son (Luke 7:11-17); and his friend Lazarus (John 11:38-44). But the life he restored to these three people was only temporary. They all died again.

Jesus was the first one *permanently* raised from the dead. He was resurrected, and he ascended to Heaven, and he will *never* die. He is alive forevermore. He is the living one, and he is the firstborn among many who will be raised to eternal life. The hope of resurrection gave early martyrs the courage to face torture and death as Christ's faithful witnesses. This same eternal hope can strengthen us as we face temptation and persecution.

Facet #3: Jesus wants his bride, the church, to know that he is the victorious ruler of the kings of the earth. Earthly rulers and dictators may try to silence the church. Government officials may persecute the church. But King Jesus is the ultimate ruler of the kings of the earth. He is King of kings and Lord of lords. He presides over the entire universe.

The Lord Jesus decides the destiny of people and nations. His empire is greater than that of Imperial Rome or Alexander's Greece or the Ottoman Empire or the British Empire or the Soviet Union or Communist China or the United States of America. His power dwarfs all the armies that ever marched and all the navies that ever sailed. He holds the title deed to every star and planet in the universe. His name is above all names.

For now, we do not see our Lord enthroned over all the nations of the world; but soon, and very soon, we *will* see the magnified majesty of our Lord Jesus Christ. We will see him in all his splendor, dominion, authority, and power.

That is why, with John the Revelator, we can say, "Come, Lord Jesus!"

And that is why the seven letters of Jesus to the seven churches of Asia Minor are so important to us today. As the world grows darker and more evil, these seven letters are our road maps through perilous times.

A LETTER OF LOST LOVE
Ephesus

George Crane was a twentieth-century psychologist and newspaper columnist. One day a woman who was furious with her husband and wanted a divorce came to Dr. Crane for counseling. She not only wanted a divorce, she said, but she also wanted to get even with her husband and cause him as much hurt and anguish as she could.

Dr. Crane listened to the woman as she sputtered and fumed, and then he gently offered her a suggestion. "Go home," he said, "and think and act as if you really love your husband. Tell him how much he means to you. Admire all his good qualities. Praise him for every decent trait. Go out of your way to be as kind, considerate, and generous as possible."

The woman was beginning to wonder whether the minister had been listening. She didn't want to be *nice* to her husband. She wanted to get *revenge!*

Then Dr. Crane explained his plan: "After you've convinced him of your undying love and that you cannot live without him, drop the bomb. Tell him how much you hate him and that you're getting a divorce."

The woman's eyes flashed with delight. She realized it was the perfect way to get her revenge. "Will he ever be surprised!" she said.

She left the office, and Dr. Crane didn't hear from her for two months. Finally, he became curious. Had she carried out the plan he had suggested? He looked up her number and called her.

When the woman answered, he asked, "Are you going to go through with the divorce?"

"Divorce?" she said. "Never! I discovered I really do love him."

When George Crane hung up the phone, he was satisfied. His plan had worked exactly as he had hoped it would. A man and a woman who had lost their first love for each other had found their love again.[1]

The Tragedy of Lost Love

The first letter Jesus sends is to the church in the city of Ephesus. It is a letter that contains words of both affirmation and warning:

To the angel of the church in Ephesus write:

These are the words of him who holds the seven
stars in his right hand and walks among the seven
golden lampstands. I know your deeds, your hard
work and your perseverance. I know that you cannot
tolerate wicked people, that you have tested those
who claim to be apostles but are not, and have found
them false. You have persevered and have endured
hardships for my name, and have not grown weary.

Yet I hold this against you: You have forsaken the love
you had at first. Consider how far you have fallen!
Repent and do the things you did at first. If you
do not repent, I will come to you and remove your
lampstand from its place. But you have this in
your favor: You hate the practices of the Nicolaitans,
which I also hate.

   Whoever has ears, let them hear what the Spirit
says to the churches. To the one who is victorious, I
will give the right to eat from the tree of life, which
is in the paradise of God.

REVELATION 2:1-7

The church, the body of all true followers of Jesus, is
the bride of Christ (see Matthew 25:1-13; Mark 2:19-20;
John 3:29; Ephesians 5:22-33; 2 Corinthians 11:2-4;
Revelation 21:2, 9-10; 22:17). The groom, the husband in

this relationship, is 100 percent faithful. (We have no doubts about the love of the faithful Lord Jesus Christ for his bride.) But the bride is another matter altogether. This bride, the church in Ephesus, had once been an ardent lover. Yet, as the years had passed, the bride's love had grown cold. It was not the same as before. At first, her love had been the passionate affection of a romantic lover. But now she seems more like a roommate than a lover.

The Ephesian bride is no longer fully in love with Jesus. She is living in the same house with him, but she is just going through the motions of marriage.

What happened to the bride's love? What stole her affections? What happened to drain the passion from her relationship with Jesus?

Other loves crept into her heart. Gradually, she began to feel a love for material things. Or a love for the world. Or a love for status. Or a love for wealth. Or a love for self.

Is such a loss *inevitable*? Are churches, or individual Christians, bound to lose their first love for Jesus? Are *all* believers doomed to experience a cooling of their desire to know, serve, and obey him? Is the tragedy of lost love in every believer's future?

Absolutely not!

In fact, I can testify—thanks to the overwhelming grace of Jesus himself—that I am more in love with Jesus today than at any other time in my life. I can't take the credit for that. Many worldly temptations have come my way through the years, but the grace and faithfulness of Jesus have enabled me to remain faithful to him—and in love with him.

The Perils of Ephesus and the Perils We Face

As we saw in the previous chapter, Ephesus, a port city on the Aegean Sea, was the first stop when sailing eastward from the island of Patmos. Because of its harbor, Ephesus was a rich center of commerce and trade. Its importance as a commercial hub would decline by the third century, because the harbor would gradually fill with silt from the river; but at the time the book of Revelation was written, Ephesus was one of the greatest cities in the ancient world, along with Athens, Rome, and Alexandria.

Ephesus was the capital of the Roman province of Asia, which encompassed most of western Asia Minor. As the seat of provincial government for a large region, Ephesus was a city of great influence in the Roman world.

Because of the nearby Temple of Artemis (completed around 550 BC), Ephesus was also a world-famous center of pagan religion. The Temple of Artemis was one of the Seven Wonders of the Ancient World, and people would travel vast distances to see it.

Ephesus was also renowned for its great buildings. One of these architectural wonders was the Library of Celsus, the third-largest library in the Greek and Roman world (next to the libraries of Alexandria and Pergamum). The Library of

Celsus may have housed as many as twelve thousand scrolls. The restored library building stands impressively amid the ruins of Ephesus today.

Another amazing structure in Ephesus was the city's huge, open-air Grand Theater, carved out of a mountainside next to the agora (marketplace). The theater seated twenty-four thousand people. It's the place where, in Acts 19:24-41, Demetrius the silversmith assembled a mob of artisans who made statuettes of the goddess Artemis. Under the apostle Paul's teaching, so many people had converted to Christ that it was hurting the business of the idol makers. They rioted and shouted, "Great is Artemis of the Ephesians!" for two hours. Paul wanted to go to the theater and speak to the mob, but his friends held him back, fearing that the mob would tear him limb from limb.

Such famous structures as the Temple of Artemis, the Library of Celsus, and the Grand Theater made Ephesus a top tourist destination in the first century. Tourism brought great wealth to the city.

The vast influence of Ephesus is why Paul founded the church there. In fact, Paul spent more time in Ephesus than in any other city during his missionary career. Just as the political and commercial worlds understood the importance of Ephesus, so Paul understood its strategic importance as a hub from which to spread the gospel, make new believers, and plant new churches.

Yet Ephesus was also a place that was unreceptive to the gospel. The pagan Roman religion had the city in its grip. It was not easy for Paul to make converts among the Ephesians—but those who did become Christ followers were deeply committed to the faith. When they got it, they *really* got it.

Paul appointed Timothy to be the pastor of the church in Ephesus. The apostle John later succeeded Timothy as pastor there. According to the second-century bishop Irenaeus, John wrote his Gospel and epistles at Ephesus.

In Revelation 2, the risen and glorified Lord Jesus directs John to deliver the first of these seven letters to John's own beloved church in Ephesus. It must have wounded John deeply to hear the Lord's words of sadness and warning directed to the Ephesian congregation.

"I Know . . ."

I love the way Jesus describes himself in the opening lines of this letter: "These are the words of him who holds the seven stars in his right hand and walks among the seven golden lampstands."

As seven is the number of completion and perfection, in holding the seven stars, Jesus is saying, in vivid symbolic language, that he is the supreme Lord over all creation. He has ultimate control over the lives of all his people. He holds the security of his people in his powerful hands. What a comfort it is to know that he holds the seven stars in his right hand. What joy and peace of mind we have!

A few years before John received this revelation from the Lord, Emperor Domitian had a series of Roman coins minted. On one side of the coin was the image of an infant boy, seated on the world, his arms outstretched, encircled by seven stars. In the Roman world, those seven stars symbolized divinity and the notion that the emperor was a god. The image represented Domitian's own son, who had died in childhood. The Latin inscription on the coin read, "The Divine Caesar, Son of the Emperor Domitian." All citizens were required to worship the image of Domitian—and this coin declared that Domitian's son, even though he was dead, was a god, a "Divine Caesar."[2]

Jesus, in his message to the church in Ephesus, may have been referring to this very image, which was stamped on the coins of the Roman Empire. The Ephesians would have been familiar with those coins. Jesus may have been saying, in effect, "Emperor Domitian claims that he is a god and his dead son was also a god. But I hold the seven stars in my right hand. I am the true and living Son of God, and I control the destiny of every human being and the destiny of empires and emperors."

Next, Jesus says to the church in Ephesus, "These are the words of him who . . . walks among the seven golden lampstands" (Revelation 2:1). What are the seven golden lampstands? They are the seven churches. When Jesus says that he walks among the seven golden lampstands, he is saying that he moves among the believers. He walks through their lives with them. For, as Jesus said during his earthly life, "where two or three gather in my name, there am I with them" (Matthew 18:20).

Jesus also gave the Ephesian believers a strong word of affirmation and encouragement: "I know your deeds, your hard work and your perseverance. I know that you cannot tolerate wicked people, that you have tested those who claim to be apostles but are not, and have found them false. You have persevered and have endured hardships for my name, and have not grown weary" (Revelation 2:2-3).

Our Lord Jesus does not overlook our hard work and perseverance. He does not take our obedience for granted. He commends us for the good work we do in his name. He commends us before he corrects us.

In each of the seven letters, Jesus says, "I know . . ." I love that! He knows, with absolute accuracy, the condition of our hearts. He knows our sincerity. He knows our sorrows. He knows our remorse over sin. He knows our plans. He knows our motives. Jesus knows us and understands us more completely than we know ourselves.

Three Virtues of Ephesus

In his letter to Ephesus, Jesus lists three virtues that the Ephesian believers exemplify. Then, sadly, he goes on to point out one heartfelt disappointment. Finally, he outlines a three-step recovery program for the church in Ephesus.

What are the three virtues of the Ephesian church?

First, the Ephesians worked hard for the sake of the gospel. Jesus says, "I know your deeds, your hard work and your perseverance" (Revelation 2:2). They were actively meeting needs and sharing the gospel. They were tireless in their service to the Lord.

Second, they were alert. "I know that you cannot tolerate wicked people, that you have tested those who claim to be apostles but are not, and have found them false" (Revelation 2:2). They were biblically sound, and they did not put up with people who tried to bring immorality or heresy into the church. They were wise and discerning (and a discerning body of believers was as rare in John's time as it is in ours). They could spot false teaching—and they rejected false teachers.

Third, they had remained steadfast through hard times and persecution. "You have persevered and have endured hardships for my name, and have not grown weary" (Revelation 2:3). They didn't complain about the unfairness of life. They faced persecution with courage, patience, and a refusal to give up. They did not grow weary. They stood their ground.

In so many ways, the Ephesian church sounds like the perfect church. The members are busy serving and working hard and defending the truth. But that's not the full story.

In their zeal for the truth, and in their eagerness to serve, they had allowed the *most important* thing to get away from them—their love for Jesus.

The Lost Love of the Ephesians

The Ephesian believers had once been deeply in love with Jesus. But over time, they had allowed their first love to grow cold.

They were like a husband who works long hours at the office but never sets aside time for romance with his wife. When she says, "We never spend time together anymore," he replies, "What do you want from me? I work hard, I'm a good provider, I bought you this beautiful home, I buy you presents, I've never been unfaithful. Why are you complaining?" But she has good reason to complain. He has lost his first love for his wife.

The Ephesians were like a wife who keeps an immaculate house—she cooks, she shops, she takes care of all the household details—but she never sits down with her husband to simply enjoy his company. They used to do so many things together, but not anymore. They used to go places together, but not anymore. She used to want to be with him more than anything else in the world, but not anymore. She has lost her first love for her husband.

We often become so absorbed in doing good things that we neglect to do the *best* and *most important* things. We do our chores and tasks, we check things off our to-do lists, we meet our financial and career goals—all the while allowing our most important relationships to fall by the wayside.

This is not a theoretical issue to me. It is deeply personal and completely real. There was a time when I placed the work of the ministry above my love for Jesus. Getting all the work done began to mean more to me than spending time with Jesus. The work I was doing was important work, it was authentic Christian service, but it had begun to replace talking to him and listening to him and basking in the warmth of his love.

In his gracious way, Jesus awakened me to the fact that I was losing my first love for him. Ever since then, I have been on my guard against falling into the snare that tripped up the Ephesians. As much as I love preaching and serving and writing and doing the work of the ministry, I need to focus so much more on my love for Jesus, on time spent alone with him.

The moment I realize that anything—*anything!*—has begun to compete with my love for Jesus, I *stop*. Whatever it is, no matter how noble, I stop instantly and immediately. Then I go to Jesus and rekindle my love for him.

This letter from Jesus tells us, in effect, "If all your service and activity does not flow from a deep love for Jesus, then stop that service, stop that activity. Just stop."

Many years ago, I was counseling a couple, and the wife shared a complaint that is all too common in marriages: "My husband never tells me he loves me anymore."

And I'll never forget the husband's reply: "I told her I loved her twenty-five years ago, and I haven't changed my mind."

This man may think he loves his wife, but if he doesn't communicate his love to her, does he *really* love her? Does he *really* care about her emotional needs? Does he love her enough to sincerely utter those three powerful words—*I love you*—every day?

How different is the love of Jesus for you and me! I confess to you that my eyes blur with tears of grateful joy as I write these words. Yes, Jesus said, "I love you," two thousand years ago when he died on the cross to save us from our sins. But he didn't just tell us once and then go silent. He didn't say, "I told you I loved you two thousand years ago and I haven't changed my mind." No, he continues to say "I love you" in a thousand different ways every day.

And all he wants is for us to love him back.

God's Broken Heart

Just as the New Testament portrays the church as the bride of Christ, the Old Testament portrays Israel as a bride who has broken the heart of her husband, the Lord.

We see God's broken heart in the book of Hosea: "When the LORD began to speak through Hosea, the LORD said to him, 'Go, marry a promiscuous woman and have children with her, for like an adulterous wife this land is guilty of unfaithfulness to the LORD'" (Hosea 1:2).

We see God's broken heart in the book of Ezekiel: "You adulterous wife! You prefer strangers to your own husband! All prostitutes receive gifts, but you give gifts to all your lovers, bribing them to come to you from everywhere for your illicit favors" (Ezekiel 16:32-33).

We see God's broken heart in the book of Jeremiah:

The word of the LORD came to me: "Go and proclaim in the hearing of Jerusalem:

"This is what the LORD says:

"'I remember the devotion of your youth,
   how as a bride you loved me
and followed me through the wilderness,
   through a land not sown.' . . .
Does a young woman forget her jewelry,
   a bride her wedding ornaments?
Yet my people have forgotten me,
   days without number."

JEREMIAH 2:1-2, 32

From these Old Testament passages, we get a sense of how God's heart must break when the church, the bride of Christ, loses its passionate love for him. When we allow our love for other things to replace our love for Jesus, we are like an unfaithful bride. His heart breaks for us as we thoughtlessly inflict still more pain on the one who went to the cross for us.

When the bride of Christ is busily working for him but has no time to talk to him or listen to him; when the bride of Christ has settled into the routine of religion instead of embracing the joyful depths of a *relationship*; when the bride of Christ has demonstrated hard work and perseverance, has guarded well against wickedness and false teachings, and has even endured hardships, but in a loveless, joyless, dispassionate way, then we in the church have forsaken the love we had at first. And we have broken the heart of Jesus.

We say we love Jesus, but really we are more in love with ourselves, with our plans and programs, with our busyness and our goals, with our biblical interpretation and our dogmas. We are no longer deeply enraptured with Jesus.

Please hear me: You and I as believers can do all the right things for the Lord. We can believe all the right things about him. We can work hard and endure hardships in his name. That's all well and good, and Jesus graciously commends us for it.

But what he longs for in our lives is our love. That's what he wants *for* us and what he wants *from* us, more than anything else. He wants our love because he is gracious, merciful, and forgiving.

Love = Time

The only way to truly love someone in a way they will feel it and know it is when you spell love T-I-M-E.

Please do not take Jesus for granted. Do not worship him only on Sundays. If the love you claim to have for him does not translate into time spent alone with him, then what you're calling *love* is not the real thing. His heart is broken when he sees that we love his blessings more than we love the one who blesses us.

We cannot read through the Old Testament without feeling the depth of God's pain over Israel's unloving heart toward him. In the same way, Jesus says to the believers in Ephesus, "I love all that you do for me, but you are neglecting the most important thing."

Always remember what the apostle Paul said to the

Corinthians—another church whose passionate first love for Jesus had cooled over time: "I am jealous for you with a godly jealousy. I promised you to one husband, to Christ, so that I might present you as a pure virgin to him. But I am afraid that just as Eve was deceived by the serpent's cunning, your minds may somehow be led astray from your sincere and pure devotion to Christ" (2 Corinthians 11:2-3).

Did you know that people can serve in the church without loving Jesus? Did you know that people can believe all the right doctrines and maintain all the correct biblical teachings, yet their love for Jesus is as cold as a butcher's meat locker? It's true.

The way you know that the love of a church or an individual believer has grown cold is when that church or that believer serves out of a sense of obligation. They believe the Bible out of a sense of duty, not out of love for Jesus. They serve out of a sense of duty, not out of love for Jesus. Their Christianity has become a burden. It has become drudgery where it was once joy unspeakable.

Do you remember your first love for Jesus?

There was a time when you would wake up in the morning and you could not wait to start the day with Jesus. But not anymore.

There was a time when you could not go through the day without telling others about Jesus and the joy of knowing him. But not anymore.

There was a time when you could not rest your head on

the pillow at night without talking to him, listening for his voice, praising him, and thanking him. But not anymore.

My friend, the divine Lover wants you back. He is calling to you. He is eager to draw you into his embrace and welcome you home.

A Three-Step Recovery Program

You may be familiar with Twelve Step addiction recovery programs. For those whose love for Jesus has grown cold, he offers a Three Step recovery program. I have worked my way through these three steps many times, and I can testify to you that it is the greatest recovery program in the world. I call it the three *R*'s: *recall, repent,* and *recapture.* This three-step recovery program comes straight from Revelation 2:5-7.

Step 1: *Recall.* Jesus says, "Consider how far you have fallen!" (Revelation 2:5). In other words, "Remember how much you used to love me—and realize how cold your love has become."

Recall those early days of faith when you were overwhelmed by your love for Jesus. Recall those early days when you were amazed by his forgiveness of sin. Recall those early days when you were astounded by the gift of eternal life.

You once loved Jesus with all your heart, soul, and mind. You couldn't thank him enough. You couldn't praise him enough. You couldn't adore him enough. You couldn't obey him enough. You couldn't cram enough of his Word into your mind. You never wanted to stop worshiping him and spending time with him.

Think back and recall: When did sin creep into your life? Who or what replaced Jesus in your affections? What distracted you? What disappointments in life caused your love for him to cool? Who or what captured your devotion? Recalling that place of failure is the first step toward recovery of your love for Jesus.

Consider how far you have fallen. Recall your first love.

Step 2: *Repent.* Jesus said, "Repent and do the things you did at first. If you do not repent, I will come to you and remove your lampstand from its place" (Revelation 2:5). To repent means to reverse course, to turn around and go in the opposite direction.

It's not enough to simply feel sorry for your sins. Many people feel sorry without repenting. Remorse is not enough. You must repent.

Step 3: *Recapture.* Jesus said, "To the one who is victorious, I will give the right to eat from the tree of life, which is in the paradise of God" (Revelation 2:7). Who are the victorious? It is those who recall their first love for Jesus, who repent of allowing that love to go cold, and who recapture what they once had in their love for the Lord.

Recalling and repenting leads us back to our first love, and it is there that we recapture what it was like in the beginning, when we first fell in love with Jesus. It is there that we will recapture the time when we used to love to worship and adore him. It is there that we will recapture the joy we felt when our love for Jesus occupied our thoughts and longings.

Why is it important to recall, repent, and then recapture our first love? If we continue in our unrepentant condition, in a state of cold and passionless love for Jesus, he will remove our lampstand. In other words, the light of Christ will be extinguished from our lives and from the life of the church. I cannot think of anything worse.

I would rather be dead than living without the light of Christ in my life. To me, the thought that Jesus might remove my lampstand is the most terrifying thought of all. I do not want to contemplate the possibility—and neither should you.

Waiting at the End of the Journey

Dr. Michael Guillen is an astrophysicist, a former ABC News science correspondent, and a Christian. In the fall of 2000, while he was with ABC News, Guillen was offered a dream assignment—a chance to be the first reporter ever to visit the sunken wreckage of the *Titanic*, almost two and a half miles below the surface of the Atlantic Ocean.

There was only one problem: Because of a traumatic experience in childhood, Guillen was terrified of the ocean depths. Despite his fears, he was determined to carry out the assignment. Calling it "the chance of a lifetime," he said, "I couldn't possibly wimp out."

So he flew to Halifax, Nova Scotia, and sailed aboard

a Russian research vessel to a location about four hundred miles from shore. Then he climbed into a Russian submersible (a small submarine), the *Mir 1*.

The cramped submersible carried three people: the Russian pilot and two passengers—Guillen and a writer from England—who had to lie stomach-down on padded benches. They could see out through nine-inch portholes. The pilot had a larger, forward-facing porthole surrounded by instruments.

Once the hatch was sealed, the crew lowered *Mir 1* into the ocean and it began its descent. Spiraling downward at a rate of about one mile per hour, the *Mir 1* took about two and a half hours to reach the ocean floor.

Within minutes after reaching the bottom, Guillen caught his first glimpse of the huge, rusting, riveted hull of the *Titanic*. It was a sobering moment, remembering all the people who had drowned when the ship sank in 1912. The pilot guided the submersible over the debris field, and Guillen was amazed at what he saw.

At one point, he saw the stern of the *Titanic*, including one of the ship's giant propellers. "It seemed to me," he recalled, "we were heading toward it too fast." In fact, the submersible was caught in a fast underwater current.

In moments, the small craft slammed into the massive propeller, then settled into the seabed. The pilot tried to move the submersible forward, backward, upward—but it was stuck. Guillen could hear the pilot communicating with the surface vessel by hydrophone, but he could not understand Russian.

Realizing that the pilot might not be able to get the submersible back to the surface, Guillen's scientific training kicked in. He began calculating how long the breathable air would last before they suffocated deep below the waves of the Atlantic.

As he thought of his dear wife, Laurel, "A heavy, crushing, depressing sadness fell upon me," he recalled. "I'd never see her again. *Never.* I couldn't believe it."

He began to contemplate death. What would it be like to die? As a Christian, he believed in the afterlife. But what would the transition from this life to the next life feel like?

About half an hour after the submersible became stuck, Guillen experienced a strange sensation. He looked around the interior of the cabin. "It was as if an invisible presence had entered it. At the same time, an uncanny and unheralded sensation of peace washed over me."

Everything became very quiet. The engine noise stopped.

Soon, Guillen realized that the submersible was rising. He called to the pilot, "Okay?"

The pilot turned, smiling, and said in a thick Russian accent, "No problem!"

Guillen now knew that they were going to live. He was going to see Laurel again. She would be waiting for him when he arrived home.

A few months later, Guillen and his wife were reading the Bible together, and they read these words from the Psalms:

If I take the wings of the morning
    and dwell in the uttermost parts of the sea,
even there your hand shall lead me,
    and your right hand shall hold me.

PSALM 139:9-10, ESV

From that moment on, he said, those words from the Bible were no longer just words. He had experienced that psalm in all its depth and meaning. He knew that God's hand really did hold him and lead him, even in the uttermost parts of the ocean. And at the end of the journey, God brought Michael Guillen safely home to his beloved wife.[3]

My friend, having a love relationship with Jesus Christ does not guarantee that your life's journey will be easy and trouble-free. There will be challenges and problems. There will be perils, and there will be suffering. There will be trials and sorrows.

But isn't it good to know that Jesus—the one who loves you, the one you love so deeply—is there in the depths of your journey? His hand will hold you and lead you. He will bring you safely home to him.

He loves you so much. Remember your first love—and return to him now.

3

A LETTER TO
A SUFFERING CHURCH
Smyrna

When Chike Uzuegbunam was growing up in Nigeria, his parents told him about a place across the ocean called America. They said it was a place where people were free to speak their minds and pursue their dreams without the government oppressing them. Eventually, Chike's family moved to America where, in 2013, he enrolled at a state-funded public college in Lawrenceville, Georgia.

It was around this same time, Chike later recalled, that he became a Christian. He called his conversion to Christ "a choice that brought me so much joy and purpose that I wanted to share my faith with as many people as possible."

He noticed that his fellow students often stood in the

many public areas around the campus, giving speeches or handing out literature in support of their political or social or environmental causes. So he decided to do as they did, to stand in a public space, "offering Christian pamphlets and engaging cheerfully with interested students." He said, "It was a chance to meet new people and respectfully share how Jesus changed my life."[1]

One day while Chike was sharing his faith in a public area, a campus security guard told him he couldn't speak publicly about his faith except in one of the college's two "speech zones," and that he would have to call ahead to reserve a time. The speech zones were open for only short periods of time each week.

He reserved a time in a speech zone, but the first time he stood up to speak, the campus police interrupted and told him he had to stop because someone had complained. According to campus policy, the school could silence any speaker who "disturbs the peace and/or comfort of person(s)."[2] In other words, anyone who claimed to be made uncomfortable by another person's speech had complete veto power over a speaker's First Amendment rights.

School officials made it clear to Chike that he could no longer publicly share his faith anywhere on campus. Other students continued to speak in public spaces about their political and social views, but talking about Jesus was banned.

So Chike consulted with attorneys from the Alliance Defending Freedom, who helped him challenge the college's speech policies in court. The college claimed that his speech wasn't a protected category of speech—even though the First Amendment expressly protects religious expression.

The district court sided with the college, so Chike's attorneys appealed. The US Court of Appeals for the Eleventh Circuit also sided with the college, but Chike and his lawyers refused to give up. They took the case all the way to the United States Supreme Court. It was there that sanity, the Constitution, and Chike Uzuegbunam finally prevailed. The high court ruled 8–1 in his favor—and in favor of Christian students at colleges and universities across the country.[3]

This doesn't mean the battle for the right of Christians to publicly share their faith has been won, once and for all. In fact, this was just one skirmish in a larger spiritual struggle that goes on and on. It is being fought in elementary schools and high schools, in corporate offices, in healthcare facilities, and in many other arenas throughout the world.

Hardly a day goes by that I don't hear of Christians being silenced or mocked or condemned or losing their careers because of their faithfulness to Christ and his Word. I could cite one example after another of individual believers and entire churches that have paid a price for standing firm against the hostile secular culture.

Things Could Get Worse

This is only my opinion—I'm not claiming any biblical authority for this statement—but unless God's people wake up in time, unless the church repents, unless we seek God more than we seek our own comfort and safety, I firmly believe that persecution will continue to get worse. Society will become more godless and wicked. Government will grow more oppressive and hostile. And we in the church—including our children and grandchildren—will soon begin to pay a heavy price.

When that happens, those who have just been playing at church, those who have been attending church to hear nice music and reassuring sermons but are not committed followers of Jesus, will fall away. They will drift into apostasy. They may even turn against Christ and join in the persecution of his committed followers.

And what about that faithful remnant—those who are serious about following Jesus despite hardship and persecution? They will learn the true meaning of his words in the Sermon on the Mount: "Blessed are those who are persecuted because of righteousness, for theirs is the kingdom of heaven. Blessed are you when people insult you, persecute you and falsely say all kinds of evil against you because of me. Rejoice and be glad, because great is your reward in heaven, for in the same way they persecuted the prophets who were before you" (Matthew 5:10-12).

Again, this is only my opinion. But I feel a burden to honestly express my heartfelt belief that things are about to get worse for the church, not better. And that's why I believe that Jesus' letter to the intensely persecuted church in Smyrna has special significance for us today.

No Rebuke for Smyrna

The church in Smyrna was one of only two churches—out of the seven—that received no word of rebuke or warning from Jesus. The other was the church at Philadelphia. The remaining five churches had to be corrected by Jesus for sins, errors, and failings.

Whether you live in the Americas, Europe, Africa, Asia, or the Middle East, the Lord's message to Smyrna is for you. Whether persecution awaits you in the future or is already your present reality, the Lord's message to Smyrna is for you. This is a message we all desperately need to hear. This is a message for every faithful Christian student, every Christian government worker, every Christian teacher, executive, preacher, or layman.

The city of Smyrna is now known as Izmir, Turkey. You can visit Izmir today and walk among the ancient ruins of Smyrna and imagine the faithful believers who lived there and received this message of blessing and encouragement from Jesus. Those long-ago believers were our brothers and sisters in the Lord, and we feel connected to them across the centuries, just as we feel connected to our present-day brothers and sisters across the oceans.

Let's hear what Jesus said to the suffering church in Smyrna:

To the angel of the church in Smyrna write:

These are the words of him who is the First and
the Last, who died and came to life again. I know
your afflictions and your poverty—yet you are rich!
I know about the slander of those who say they are
Jews and are not, but are a synagogue of Satan. Do
not be afraid of what you are about to suffer. I tell
you, the devil will put some of you in prison to test
you, and you will suffer persecution for ten days. Be
faithful, even to the point of death, and I will give
you life as your victor's crown.

Whoever has ears, let them hear what the Spirit
says to the churches. The one who is victorious will
not be hurt at all by the second death.

REVELATION 2:8-11

In the previous chapter, we saw that the church in Ephesus
was biblically sound, but they had lost their first love for
Jesus. The Ephesians were busy for Jesus, and they believed
the right things, but their busyness was not driven by a deep
and heartfelt love for Jesus.

In Smyrna, the believers have maintained their passion for
Jesus—even in hard times, even under the broiling heat of
persecution. In fact, the believers in Smyrna seem to exemplify a principle I have observed again and again: When your
love for Jesus is real, it will bring you suffering. As the apostle
Paul observed, "Everyone who wants to live a godly life in
Christ Jesus will be persecuted" (2 Timothy 3:12).

The Deeply Religious Pagans of Smyrna

The city of Smyrna was located about thirty-five miles north of Ephesus. Smyrna was a great trading city—called "the Ornament of Asia" and "the Crown of Asia" because of its beauty. Smyrna was founded circa 1000 BC as an Aeolian Greek colony. Around 600 BC, the army of King Alyattes of Lydia completely destroyed Smyrna. The site remained desolate for four hundred years, until Alexander the Great ordered the rebuilding of the city.

When Smyrna was rebuilt, the designers created broad, well-paved avenues laid out in a grid. The main street is believed to have stretched from the temple of the god Zeus at one end of the city to the temple of the mother goddess Cybele at the other.

In 197 BC, the people of Smyrna wanted to join the increasingly powerful empire of Rome. To impress the Roman government and show their love for Roman culture, the citizens of Smyrna invented a new religion, the cult of the goddess they called Roma, who represented the spirit of the Roman Empire. Despite this flattery, Rome did not immediately adopt Smyrna as a colony.

In 133 BC, when King Attalus III of Pergamum died, his will stated that the entire region of Asia should be handed over to Rome. The Romans organized this land into a province— the Roman province of Asia—and Smyrna became a major Roman seaport.

The people of Smyrna were deeply religious. Not only did they build a great temple for their newly invented goddess Roma, but they built temples for every other god and goddess they could think of. They weren't taking any chances. They made sure to worship every miserable deity in the Greek and Roman pantheons. Every time they heard of a new god, they built another temple. The only deity they rejected was the one true God.

The Christian "Atheists" of Smyrna

Here is the ultimate irony of these deeply religious citizens of Smyrna: Because the Christians rejected all the many pagan gods out of faithfulness to the one true God, the pagan people of Smyrna called the Christians "atheists."

One of the most famous Christians in Smyrna was Polycarp (AD 69–155), who was a disciple of John. Polycarp served as the bishop of Smyrna until his arrest during a time of persecution in the second century. When Polycarp was taken before the Roman governor to be judged, the governor said, "Consider your age, and be sensible. Swear and say, 'Down with the atheists.'"

The governor meant "down with the Christians," but Polycarp knew that Christians were not atheists. So with a clear conscience, he said, "Down with the atheists."

The governor decided to give Polycarp another test. "Swear, reproach Christ," he said, "and I will release you."

But this Polycarp would not do. "Eighty and six years

have I served him," the old bishop replied, "and he never once wronged me; how then shall I blaspheme my King, Who hath saved me?"[4]

History records that the faithful Polycarp was burned at the stake.

Almost two thousand years before George Orwell, the pagans in Smyrna were using Orwellian terminology, turning the meaning of words inside out, labeling Christianity "atheism."

You may recall that Orwell, in his novel *1984*, introduced us to the Ministry of Truth, whose purpose was to spread lies and propaganda. On the side of the huge, white pyramid that housed the Ministry of Truth was this inscription: "War is peace. Freedom is slavery. Ignorance is strength."

Long before Orwell warned us about the abuse of language, Satan was manipulating words to confuse the masses. And Satan has not changed his tactics over time. He is still the god of confusion and the father of lies. He is constantly trying to make it impossible for people to distinguish falsehood from truth. We can see Satan's hand in the confusion of the meanings of words today.

In American academic circles, positive-sounding (but Orwellian) buzzwords are used to disguise a sinister reality. As an opinion piece from the American Enterprise Institute observed, "Unfortunately, in higher education, 'Diversity, Equity, and Inclusion (DEI)' has taken on an Orwellian aspect—becoming a tool of 'groupthink, censorship, and exclusion.'"[5]

One of the most sinister abuses of language today is in the realm of transgender activism. Trans activists want to take dysphoric children away from their parents, convince them they are a different gender, and chemically or surgically mutilate them. To disguise their horrifying agenda behind positive-sounding words, they call it "gender-affirming care," though it is hardly *affirming* or *caring*. Anyone who opposes such doublespeak, and the evil intentions behind it is vilified as "transphobic."

Do you see how they distort the language to intimidate and control? I urge you to stand up to these people. Challenge their deceptive use of words. Reject their dishonest vocabulary.

If you meet a person who is gender-confused and who identifies as a "trans man" or a "trans woman," you should always be gracious and polite. Treat that person with respect and caring, just as Jesus would. But in the realm of political and social dialogue, never yield an inch to the satanic agenda of the trans activists.

As hostility and persecution increase around the world, we can expect to see the enemies of Christianity continue to subvert the meaning of words to sow confusion and lies. The Satan-inspired pagans did this to the Christians in Smyrna. We should not be surprised when it happens to us as well.

Two Comforting Words: "I Know"

The risen and glorified Lord Jesus begins by telling the believers in Smyrna who he is: "These are the words of him who is the First and the Last, who died and came to life again" (Revelation 2:8). Why does Jesus identify himself this way? Don't the Christians in Smyrna know who he is? Don't they know he is the First and the Last, the Alpha and the Omega, the one who died and rose again?

Of course they do. But in the midst of their suffering, they needed to be reminded. We, too, need to be reminded every day of who our Lord and Savior truly is.

Jesus says, "I am the Alpha and the Omega, the First and the Last, the Beginning and the End" (Revelation 22:13). Alpha is the first letter in the Greek alphabet and Omega is the last. Jesus is the A and the Z and everything in between. He is the only one who has defeated death and the grave—and he will give us power over death. This great truth makes us fearless. It gives us the unbreakable courage to face death and say, "Bring it on!" because we have confidence in the one who has defeated death.

The two most comforting words in this letter, whether in the first century or the twenty-first century, are "I know."

"*I know* your afflictions . . ."

"*I know* about the slander . . ."

These two words fill me with joy, confidence, comfort, and peace. Jesus is saying, in effect, "*I know* you are being falsely accused and deliberately misunderstood. *I know* the price you are paying for your faithfulness. *I know* what Satan is doing to you and your family and your business and your reputation." In times of trial and suffering, it is comforting to remember that *Jesus knows.*

What does Jesus mean when he says, "I know about the slander of those who say they are Jews and are not, but are a synagogue of Satan" (Revelation 2:9)?

The Christians in Smyrna were not only being persecuted by the pagan idol-worshipers. They were also hated by many Jews in the city.

You'll recall that when Domitian ascended to the throne, he gave himself the title *Dominus et Deus*, "Lord and God," and demanded to be worshiped as a god. The Romans tolerated the Jews and their religion because they saw Judaism as an ethnically Jewish faith. The Jews were not trying to convert Romans to their religion. As a result, the Jews received an exemption from having to sacrifice and chant praise to the image of the emperor; they were allowed, instead, to sacrifice and pray to their own God on behalf of the emperor.[6]

But the Romans didn't recognize the newly founded Christian faith. They were suspicious of these Christians who were preaching a new gospel and making converts by the thousands. The Romans feared that Christianity might destabilize the empire. As a result, Christians were subjected to a severe loyalty test: The Romans required Christians to sacrifice and pray to the image of Domitian and call him "Lord and God"—something no sincere Christian could ever do.

So the Christians faced official persecution by the Roman government for refusing to obey the law regarding the worship of the emperor. To make matters worse, some in the Jewish community in Smyrna were bitterly opposed to Christianity—and they were apparently reporting the

Christians to the Roman officials. These Jewish opponents told the Romans that the Christians gave their allegiance to another king instead of Domitian—and that, of course, was true. The Christians worshiped King Jesus.

But these Jewish opponents were also telling lies about the Christians. That's why Jesus said, "I know about the slander of those who say they are Jews and are not, but are a synagogue of Satan" (Revelation 2:9). (The Greek word for "slander" in that statement is *blasphemeō*.) What were the lies and slanders the Jewish enemies spread? We can't be certain, but it's likely they told the Roman authorities that the Christians were plotting a rebellion against Roman rule.[7]

These kinds of slanders were not new. In the book of Acts, a sect of Jews in Thessalonica spread lies against the apostle Paul, inciting a riot and shouting, "These men who have caused trouble all over the world have now come here. . . . They are all defying Caesar's decrees, saying that there is another king, one called Jesus" (Acts 17:6-7). So the Jewish faction in Smyrna probably spread similar rumors about the believers in that city. As a result, many Christians in Smyrna were being arrested and imprisoned on false charges.

A Synagogue of Satan

When Jesus calls these Jewish opponents "a synagogue of Satan," he doesn't mean they worship the devil. He means they are unwittingly doing Satan's bidding. They have been duped into carrying out Satan's agenda.

We see a similar principle in Matthew 16. There, Jesus is teaching the disciples that he would have to go to Jerusalem and be killed. Peter took Jesus aside and said, "Never, Lord! . . . This shall never happen to you!" (Matthew 16:22). And Jesus turned to Peter and said, "Get behind me, Satan! You are a stumbling block to me; you do not have in mind the concerns of God, but merely human concerns" (Matthew 16:23). Jesus was not literally calling Peter *Satan*, but he was forcefully making a point: Peter, in his bumbling and well-meaning way, was not serving God's purpose but was unwittingly helping Satan's plans. He was trying to prevent Jesus from going to the cross—but Jesus had to suffer crucifixion and death to fulfill the plan of God the Father.

In a similar way, these deeply religious Jews—who, in their own limited understanding, were zealous for God—were actually doing Satan's bidding. They were spreading lies concocted by the father of lies. They were spreading slanders invented by the author of confusion and the accuser of the saints. That is why Jesus called them "a synagogue of Satan" (Revelation 2:9).

Satan's ultimate goal was to silence the believers in Smyrna. The devil does not want Christians to testify to the power of Jesus working in them. So he will slander Christians if he can. He will paralyze them with fear if he can. He will persecute and martyr Christians if that's what it takes.

And make no mistake: Satan wants to silence you.

So I have a question for you: What would it take for Satan to silence you? Has he intimidated you into silence? Has he made you afraid to witness for Jesus? What are the fears you struggle with? Fear of rejection? Fear of being mocked or criticized? Fear of being falsely accused?

Fear is the great silencer of believers. And Jesus wants us to know that the antidote to fear is faith. He spoke peace to the fears of the believers in Smyrna. He said, "I know your afflictions. . . . Do not be afraid of what you are about to suffer" (Revelation 2:9-10).

Whatever you are going through, whatever fears you are facing, Jesus knows your afflictions. Don't be afraid. Have faith and confidence in him.

The key thought that unlocks this entire letter is the line that reads, "Be faithful, even to the point of death, and I will give you life as your victor's crown" (Revelation 2:10). The word *faithful* is derived from the word *faith*. To be faithful is to cling to faith. It means to hold on to your absolute trust in Jesus and confidence in his promises.

Why were the believers in Smyrna hated by the world? Because they were faithful in their trust in Jesus and their love for Jesus. And because they were hated, they were persecuted. And because they were persecuted, they loved Jesus even more.

They had confidence in the one who is the First and the Last, who died and came to life again. There is nothing that frightens away fear like the reality of who Jesus is. Nothing banishes fear like the power of the resurrected Jesus. Nothing replaces fear with faith like confidence in the one who conquered death.

Why Do People Hate the Gospel?

The gospel of Jesus Christ is the story of God's boundless love for us. It's the story of how God sent his Son to die in our place so that we might be forgiven—and live forever with him. There is no greater story than the gospel story.

And yet we are surrounded in every corner of our culture by people who hate the gospel of Jesus Christ. They're not merely indifferent to the gospel. They *hate* it! Have you ever wondered why? Why do some people become angry, bitter, and rude whenever the Good News of Jesus is mentioned in their presence?

The answer: The gospel of Jesus Christ exposes our sin and our guilt. It strips away our excuses and our false self-righteousness. Those who have not received new life through faith in Jesus Christ do not want their sin and guilt exposed. They don't want to be reminded of God's holy judgment. They don't want to be told that they are helpless to save themselves.

The Bible has a term for such a person: "the natural man." As Paul wrote to the Corinthians, "The natural man does not receive the things of the Spirit of God, for they are foolishness to him; nor can he know them, because they are spiritually discerned" (1 Corinthians 2:14, NKJV).

The natural man or natural woman says, "I am the captain of my own life and the master of my own soul. I don't need the cross of Jesus. I have everything under control."

And here's the real tragedy of the natural man and natural woman who feel no need for Jesus: Many of them are in churches. You may wonder, "How can this be? Why would people who have no use for the gospel attend church?"

The answer is simple: Many churches do not preach the gospel. Many churches are designed for the care and comfort of the natural man and woman. Many preachers have watered down the gospel to make it acceptable to the natural man and woman. These preachers and these churches want to fit in with the world, so they have abandoned the gospel. They preach a feel-good "gospel" of self-help, of doing good works, of having high self-esteem.

The fact that someone could sit in church week after week and never hear the true gospel saddens me—and I could name dozens of such churches. And I know this is a tragedy that breaks the heart of Jesus.

The Power, Knowledge, and Purpose of Jesus

The resurrected and glorified Lord Jesus delivered these seven letters to the seven churches because he wants all his faithful followers to know they do not need to be frightened. They can live faithfully and fearlessly. Why? Three reasons: (1) Jesus alone has all the power; (2) Jesus alone knows all things; (3) Jesus alone has a purpose in everything.

Let's look at each of these three reasons for our confidence in Jesus.

1. *Jesus alone has all the power.* When he says, "I am the Alpha and the Omega, the First and the Last, the Beginning

and the End" (Revelation 22:13), he is reminding us that he alone has the power that created the heavens and the earth. He alone has the power to lay down his life and take it up again.

Jesus is saying, in effect, "I was there before the Creation, and I'm going to be there when it's all destroyed. No one comes before me, and no one comes after me. I created it all. I control it all. I died and they thought it was all finished. But on the third day I rose again. I have defeated the most powerful enemy of all. Remember that whenever you feel afraid or timid."

Whenever you are facing affliction and suffering, remember that Jesus has all the power. Remember that he has all the power when you are battling temptation. Remember that he has all the power when you are slandered and falsely accused. Remember that he has all the power when you face the final enemy, death itself.

2. *Jesus alone knows all things.* He not only knows what troubles you, he also knows the way through your afflictions. You may not always feel his grip, but he is holding your hand.

When Jesus says, "I know," he is saying that no matter how baffling and painful your trial may be, he's been there. He knows what it feels like. He knows what you are going through. People might call you poor, but he calls you rich. People might call you ignorant, but he calls you wise. People might slander you for your faith, but Jesus will exalt you. Do not listen to the false accusations of the enemy. Jesus knows the truth.

3. *Jesus alone has a purpose in everything.* He even has a purpose for the trials and suffering in your life. He says, "Do not be afraid of what you are about to suffer. I tell you, the devil will put some of you in prison to test you, and you will suffer persecution for ten days. Be faithful, even to the point of death, and I will give you life as your victor's crown" (Revelation 2:10).

Why did Jesus say that the Christians in Smyrna would "suffer persecution for ten days"? This is not a literal number of days. It means their suffering will last for only a limited time. It will not go on forever. The Lord may allow evil to prosper for a while, but only so that the coming judgment will be greater.

What Satan means for evil Jesus will transform into good. Satan will try to destroy us, but Jesus will turn all of Satan's curses into blessings.

Jesus has promised that we are totally secure in the palm of his hand. He said, "I give them eternal life, and they shall never perish; no one will snatch them out of my hand. My Father, who has given them to me, is greater than all; no one can snatch them out of my Father's hand" (John 10:28-29).

Satan is powerless to destroy us—as hard as he may try. He can fill our enemies with hate and provoke them to lie about us and slander us. But all their persecution and false accusations and lies will amount to nothing, because we are safe in the strong hands of Jesus.

A LETTER TO THE CHURCH NEAR SATAN'S THRONE
Pergamum

Just before midnight on Friday, December 29, 1972, Eastern Air Lines Flight 401 from New York was approaching Miami International Airport. As the plane descended and the first officer lowered the landing gear, he noticed a problem. The green indicator light for the nose gear did not light up.

There were two possible explanations: either the nose gear had malfunctioned, or the bulb in the indicator light had burned out. But there was no way to tell for sure. The cockpit crew tried raising and lowering the gear, but the indicator light remained dark.

The crew radioed the tower and informed the approach controller that they had to abort the landing. The controller told Flight 401 to climb to two thousand feet and fly a holding pattern over the Florida Everglades.

As the plane traveled in an oval-shaped pattern, the crew tried to figure out whether the nose gear was actually down. The first officer placed the aircraft on autopilot so that he and the crew could focus on making sure the landing gear was in position. The plane continued flying level at two thousand feet for about eighty seconds.

At that point, someone accidentally bumped the controls and turned off the autopilot. Though the plane continued to fly smoothly, no one was at the controls. The autopilot no longer controlled the altitude, and the cockpit crew was focused on the indicator light and landing gear.

No one noticed when the plane descended to 1,800 feet, where it proceeded to fly level for about two minutes. Then the plane dropped an additional three hundred feet in a little over a minute. The descent was so smooth, so gradual, that the crew didn't notice. It felt exactly as if the autopilot were controlling the plane.

As the plane continued its descent, a warning chime sounded on the engineer's instrument panel—but the engineer wasn't there to hear it. He was belowdecks checking on the nose gear.

Another minute passed. The plane was at one thousand feet of altitude and still descending. Soon it was time for the plane to make another turn in its holding pattern. The first officer looked at the controls in alarm. The cockpit voice recorder captured the conversation.

"We did something to the altitude," the first officer said.

The captain said, "What?"

"We're still at two thousand feet, right?"

The captain shouted, "Hey—what's happening here?"

Nine seconds later, Flight 401 smashed into the Everglades at more than two hundred miles per hour. The left wing sliced into the swamp first, then the body of the aircraft splashed down and crashed through trees and muddy waters, flying apart as it went.

In all, one hundred one people died, including the entire cockpit crew. Miraculously, seventy-five people survived the disaster.

This horrifying event was set in motion by the failure of a $12 lightbulb. But the real cause of the tragedy was that no one realized the plane had drifted off course while the cockpit crew was distracted. The descent was so smooth and gradual that no one realized the plane was headed for destruction.[1]

In the third letter in Revelation, we find that the church in Pergamum was also on a glide path to doom. Outwardly, it seemed like everything was fine. The believers were faithful to Jesus, despite intense persecution. They were making converts and preaching in his name.

But there was a problem at the heart of the church at Pergamum. The believers had become inattentive and were drifting from the truth. The descent into error was so smooth and gradual that no one realized that destruction lay ahead.

So Jesus delivers a message of warning—a warning that you and I would be wise to heed.

"I Know Where You Live"

The Greek city of Pergamum (or Pergamon) was about one hundred miles north of Ephesus and fifty miles north of Smyrna. Pergamum was built on a high promontory about a thousand feet above the plain and about sixteen miles inland from the Aegean coastline. The Turkish city of Bergama now spreads out on the plain southeast of the ruins of Pergamum.

Pergamum was the regional center for the imperial cult, the worship of the Roman emperor. In neighboring cities, the people were obligated by law to offer a sacrifice to the emperor once a year. But in Pergamum, the people offered a daily sacrifice to the emperor. The Christians in Pergamum were expected to conform to these practices—and when they refused to conform, they suffered intense persecution from the Roman government and the pagan cultists.

Here is the letter the risen and glorified Lord Jesus sent to the believers in Pergamum:

> To the angel of the church in Pergamum write:
>   These are the words of him who has the sharp, double-edged sword. I know where you live—where Satan has his throne. Yet you remain true to my name. You did not renounce your faith in me, not even in the days of Antipas, my faithful witness, who was put to death in your city—where Satan lives.
>   Nevertheless, I have a few things against you: There are some among you who hold to the

teaching of Balaam, who taught Balak to entice the Israelites to sin so that they ate food sacrificed to idols and committed sexual immorality. Likewise, you also have those who hold to the teaching of the Nicolaitans. Repent therefore! Otherwise, I will soon come to you and will fight against them with the sword of my mouth.

Whoever has ears, let them hear what the Spirit says to the churches. To the one who is victorious, I will give some of the hidden manna. I will also give that person a white stone with a new name written on it, known only to the one who receives it.

REVELATION 2:12-17

As he previously said to the believers in Ephesus and Smyrna, Jesus again says, "I know." To the believers in Pergamum, he says, "I know where you live."

Those words can either be a blessing or a threat. Many years ago, when I was working on my doctoral dissertation, I had to interview some Muslim extremists. These were dangerous people, and I was nervous about the encounter—and with good reason. When I sat down to interview them, the first thing they said to me was, "Write down exactly what we tell you— because we know where you live." Now *that* was a *threat*.

I was terrified. The thought of what they might do to me kept me awake several nights. And of this you can be sure: I wrote down *exactly* what they told me. Why? Because they told me they knew where I lived.

What a different tone and feeling Jesus brings to these words. When he says, "I know where you live," it's a loving, caring statement. He has compassion for the believers in Pergamum. He has empathy for them. He understands their circumstances, their fears, and their temptations. He knows the evil forces that surround them.

Where Satan Has His Throne

Jesus tells the believers in Pergamum, "I know where you live—where Satan has his throne" (Revelation 2:13). What did he mean? What was Satan's throne?

At the time that John wrote the book of Revelation, Pergamum was a major cultural and religious center. The city featured a spacious theater carved out of a hillside, athletic facilities, pagan temples, pagan religious shrines, and the second largest library in the world (surpassed only by that of Alexandria in Egypt).

The largest religious shrine in Pergamum was the Great Altar of Zeus, built in the second century BC. This massive altar, roughly thirty-five yards wide, was a center of Greek and Roman religious activity. The priests of Zeus made sacrifices at the altar day and night.

If not for a German engineer and archaeologist named Carl Humann, we might know very little about the Altar of Zeus and other buildings from ancient Pergamum. During the 1860s, Humann went to Pergamum and worked with the Ottoman Turkish government to preserve the city's antiquities.

When Humann arrived, he saw that townspeople from Bergama were chopping up the marble ruins and burning the marble to produce lime for mortaring bricks. Humann brought in archaeologists to help him identify, preserve, and reconstruct the ruins, including the ruins of the Altar of Zeus. He arranged to ship the Altar in fragments to Germany, where it would be pieced together like a jigsaw puzzle.

The reconstructed Altar is now a majestic display in the Pergamon Museum in Berlin. Many Christian scholars believe that the Great Altar of Zeus is what Jesus refers to when he says that Pergamum is "where Satan has his throne."

But I don't believe Jesus was referring only to the Altar of Zeus. Pergamum was also the center for the worship of the god Asclepius, the ancient Greek god of healing. The pagans believed Asclepius was the son of Apollo. He is depicted in Greek and Roman art as a bearded man with a wooden staff, with a serpent entwined around the staff.

The staff and snake of Asclepius, called the caduceus, has been adopted as a symbol of the practice of medicine. The temple of Asclepius was called the Asclepieion. There, the pagan people of Pergamum would bring their sick to bathe in its pools and fountains, and (if they were fortunate) to be touched by one of the nonvenomous snakes that slithered in the halls and rooms of the Asclepieion. The pagans believed that if they were touched by one of the temple snakes, they were touched by Asclepius himself.

The practice of medicine in those days was primitive by

our standards and had more to do with sorcery than science. To the pagans, Asclepius represented health and healing. But to the Christians in Pergamum, the serpent cult of Asclepius was a reminder of Satan who crawled into the Garden of Eden as a snake.

Among Christians, Jesus is the Great Physician, because he said, "It is not the healthy who need a doctor, but the sick. I have not come to call the righteous, but sinners" (Mark 2:17). He came to cure the sick in body, soul, and spirit. Because the Pergamum church taught that Jesus, not Asclepius, is the Great Physician, the cult of Asclepius hated and persecuted the Christians.

For these reasons, Jesus said that Pergamum is "where Satan has his throne."

A Church that Tolerated Sin

Jesus affirms the courage and early faithfulness of the believers in Pergamum. "Yet you remain true to my name," he says. "You did not renounce your faith in me, not even in the days of Antipas, my faithful witness, who was put to death in your city—where Satan lives" (Revelation 2:13).

Who was Antipas? According to tradition, Antipas was the bishop of Pergamum during the brutal reign of the Roman emperor Nero. He was probably ordained to that position by the apostle John himself. Ancient accounts indicate that Antipas was martyred by being burned alive in a bull-shaped brass altar. His "crime," according to these accounts, was that he cast out demons through prayer—demons that were prized and worshiped by the pagan people of Pergamum.

We tend to think of the Greek and Roman gods as a bunch of lifeless marble statues. But the truth is that demons, sorcery, and witchcraft were very much a part of those ancient pagan religions.

The Temple of Trajan, built in honor of an earlier Roman emperor, dominated the city and served as the gathering place for the imperial cult. In Pergamum, pagan rituals and Roman political power combined to create a spiritually oppressive atmosphere for the Christian community. The emperor worship in Pergamum gives us an idea of the kind of worship the Antichrist will demand from the entire human race in the last days.

The risen and glorified Jesus affirmed the believers in Pergamum. Even though they lived in the city where Satan had his throne, Jesus said, "You did not renounce your faith in me" (Revelation 2:13).

Unfortunately, the Lord's message to the church at Pergamum doesn't stop there. He goes on to say, "Nevertheless, I have a few things against you" (Revelation 2:14).

Like the cockpit crew of that ill-fated airliner, the Christians in Pergamum had lost their focus on what really mattered. They thought they were flying straight and level—and they were completely unaware that they were on a gradual downward path to destruction.

Where had they gone wrong? What was the error these Christians had fallen into? Outwardly, the church in Pergamum seemed to be doing fine. The believers stood firmly and faithfully against persecution. It was a growing church. Other pastors in the region might have even envied the Pergamum church for its vigor and its courage.

But there was a problem that these believers were ignoring, and the problem was growing increasingly more dangerous and urgent: The church in Pergamum was tolerating sin and false teaching.

"There are some among you," Jesus says, "who hold to the teaching of Balaam, who taught Balak to entice the Israelites to sin so that they ate food sacrificed to idols and committed sexual immorality" (Revelation 2:14). The church in Pergamum was accepting sexually immoral people into membership and even leadership. These sexually immoral church members were so blatant about their sin that they were luring other church members into immoral practices.

Picture a church with a culturally relevant message being proclaimed from the pulpit, a great music program, a growing children's ministry, a strong outreach to the community. This church is not denying Christ—in fact, this church has withstood persecution from hostile groups and even the government. It's a growing church that is attracting many new members. Outwardly, this is a great church, an amazing church.

But inwardly, the church is tolerating immorality. The people see a few church members practicing an immoral way of life, and they say, "Well, that's an alternate lifestyle. Who are we to judge?"

That is what the church at Pergamum was like.

Clogged Spiritual Arteries

Jim Fixx was an American runner and the author of the 1977 bestseller *The Complete Book of Running.* He is credited with launching the running and fitness craze of the late 1970s and 1980s.

When Fixx started running in 1967, he was thirty-five years old, weighed 214 pounds, and was a two-pack-a-day smoker. By the time he published *The Complete Book of Running,* he had shed sixty pounds and completely quit smoking. He made numerous appearances on TV and radio talk shows, preaching the benefits of exercise.

On July 20, 1984, as he was taking his daily run along a Vermont road, Fixx suffered a massive heart attack and died almost instantly. Even though he was a regular runner committed to improving his physical fitness, the autopsy showed that one of his coronary arteries was completely blocked and another was 80 percent blocked. The coroner also found signs that Fixx had suffered previous heart attacks that had gone undiagnosed.[2]

Much like Jim Fixx, the church in Pergamum was seemingly healthy and vital on the outside, but with a ticking time bomb on the inside. The believers in Pergamum suffered from clogged spiritual arteries. They couldn't diagnose themselves. They needed intervention from the all-knowing, all-seeing Great Physician.

The eyes of Jesus are a million times more powerful than the most sensitive magnetic resonance imaging machine. And his diagnosis of the believers at Pergamum was not only that they tolerated sin in their midst, but that they also tolerated false, heretical teaching. Jesus says, "Likewise, you also have those who hold to the teaching of the Nicolaitans. Repent therefore! Otherwise, I will soon come to you and will fight against them with the sword of my mouth" (Revelation 2:15-16).

The church at large has been commanded to take new ground for the Kingdom of God. But the church in America seems to be losing ground. It seems to be retreating, not advancing. One reason for the decline of the American church may be that some churches have been following the Pergamum model. Perhaps some of those failed churches have tolerated sin and false teaching—and the Lord has chosen to weed them out.

Lifeway Research reports that American Protestant churches are closing their doors in increasing numbers. The report cited a study showing that in 2019, three thousand new churches opened while 4,500 churches closed—a net loss of 1,500 churches in a single year. That was the last year for which statistics were available, but Lifeway Research projected that this trend would likely accelerate in the years to come.

Scott McConnell, executive director at Lifeway Research, said, "In the last three years, all signs are pointing to a continued pace of closures probably similar to 2019 or possibly higher, as there's been a really rapid rise in American individuals who say they're not religious."[3]

I'm sure there are many reasons for the decline of the American church, not just one. The fact that one church struggles and eventually must close its doors is not proof that there was a toleration for sin and error in that church. But I can't help thinking that at least part of the reason for the decline of churches in America is that many American churches are like the church at Pergamum.

Could it be that at least *some* of the churches that have fallen by the wayside—churches that once *seemed* strong and healthy on the outside—were suffering from spiritually clogged arteries on the inside? Could it be that some of these churches have tolerated sin and heretical doctrine—and that they have been judged and removed by the sword of Jesus' mouth?

The resurrected and glorified Lord Jesus pleads with the church at Pergamum—and he pleads with you and me: Stop tolerating sin. Stop making excuses for immorality. Stop rationalizing worldly heresies. It's time to judge the sin in our midst—in our congregations and in ourselves—before it destroys the church.

If you look closely at the Lord's warnings to the church at Pergamum, you can discern a three-part structure. First, the Great Physician diagnoses the sickness at the heart of the church. Second, the Great Physician expresses disappointment in what he has found. Third, the Great Physician must make a decision about the sickness in the church. In short, the letter is about the Lord's *diagnosis*, his *disappointment*, and his *decision*.

The Great Physician's Diagnosis

Though the believers in Pergamum have held fast to their faith that Jesus died for their sin and rose again, though they have never denied the name of Jesus, though they have endured persecution for his sake, the church is unhealthy. These believers are undergoing a physical exam, and the Great Physician says, "Blood pressure, good. Pulse, normal. Temperature, normal. Let me listen to your heart. . . . Uh-oh."

No one wants to hear the doctor say, "Uh-oh."

In verses 14 and 15, Jesus gives us the diagnosis: "Nevertheless, I have a few things against you: There are some among you who hold to the teaching of Balaam, who taught Balak to entice the Israelites to sin so that they ate food sacrificed to idols and committed sexual immorality. Likewise, you also have those who hold to the teaching of the Nicolaitans."

The Lord's diagnosis is serious: The patient tolerates sin and error.

The Great Physician's Disappointment

We can hear the disappointment in his voice as he lays out the diagnosis. The church at Pergamum has fallen into a trap that has ensnared countless churches right up to the present day. They know there is sin and heresy in their midst, yet they refuse to judge the sin and expel the heresy.

Jesus tells the believers in Pergamum, "There are some among you who hold to the teaching of Balaam, who taught Balak to entice the Israelites to sin." The story of Balaam is found in Numbers 22–24. When King Balak of Moab heard that the Israelites were traveling through his land, he hired a sorcerer named Balaam to curse the Israelites—but God intervened and caused Balaam to bless the Israelites instead.

Later, when Balaam realized that God would not allow him to curse the people of Israel, he came up with a diabolical plan. He advised King Balak to tempt the Hebrew nation into immorality and the idolatrous worship of Baal. King Balak followed Balaam's advice, and many Israelite men were lured into immoral acts with the women of Moab and into the worship of Baal (Numbers 25:1-9; 31:16).

As punishment, God sent a plague into the Israelite camp that left twenty-four thousand dead.

That is what Jesus meant regarding the teaching of Balaam, a sobering story from the Old Testament. Then, in New Testament times, came another dangerous false teaching, as Jesus warned: "Likewise, you also have those who hold to the teaching of the Nicolaitans" (Revelation 2:15).

The Bible doesn't tell us what the Nicolaitans believed and practiced, but the context indicates they preached a doctrine of lawlessness. It's reasonable to assume they claimed that Christians, not being under the Law, were not bound by any moral rules or restrictions.

The Nicolaitans had tried to infiltrate the church at Ephesus, but the Ephesians (unlike the believers in Pergamum) had expelled the Nicolaitans and their false teachings. As we have seen, Jesus affirmed the Ephesians, saying, "But you have this in your favor: You hate the practices of the Nicolaitans, which I also hate" (Revelation 2:6).

The Nicolaitans were also mentioned (and condemned) by some of the early church fathers, including Irenaeus, Tertullian, and Clement of Alexandria. The toleration of sin and heresy in the church is still a life-and-death issue for churches in the twenty-first century. I have seen the evidence of this sickness with my own eyes.

I have often heard people who refuse to condemn sin rationalize their tolerance by quoting the words of Jesus out of context: "Do not judge, or you too will be judged" (Matthew 7:1). But the rest of that statement (which people frequently leave out) reads, "For in the same way you judge others, you will be judged, and with the measure you use, it will be measured to you" (Matthew 7:2).

Jesus is not saying that we should never be discerning about sin. He's not saying we should tolerate wickedness in ourselves or others. Clearly, he is warning us not to be hypocritical. We should not pass judgment on others while ignoring our own sins. We need to purify our hearts and our motives before we seek to discern the sinful actions of others.

The apostle Paul wrote about the importance of

discernment—that is, having sober judgment regarding the seriousness of sin. He prayed for the Philippians that they might "be able to discern what is best and may be pure and blameless for the day of Christ" (Philippians 1:10). And he told the church in Galatia, "Brothers and sisters, if someone is caught in a sin, you who live by the Spirit should restore that person gently. But watch yourselves, or you also may be tempted" (Galatians 6:1).

When we become aware that sin has infected the church, we are to *act*, we are to *speak*, we are to *gently* restore the sinner to the path of righteousness. And we must do so in all humility, fully aware that we ourselves are prone to temptation and sin.

If we turn a blind eye to the growing health crisis in the church, there will come a time when we must submit to the scalpel of the Great Physician. We'll have to face the consequences of our lazy tolerance of sin and error in the church.

When people say, "We shouldn't be judgmental toward the sins of others," you can take it as a dead giveaway that they are not judging—and repenting of—their own sin. Whenever people are afraid to call sin by its rightful name, you can be certain it's because they are harboring sin in their own lives.

Whenever there is a hidden sin; whenever there is unconfessed sin; whenever there is a cherished sin; whenever there is a rationalized sin, we only compound the problem by spreading moral confusion: "Oh, we shouldn't be judgmental. Nobody's perfect. We're all human, right?"

Don't fall for those flimsy excuses and self-justifications. Judging sin must always begin with judging ourselves, examining ourselves, confessing our sins—and completely repenting of those sins.

The Great Physician's Decision

After diagnosing the hidden health problems of the Pergamum believers, after expressing his disappointment that they have neglected their spiritual health, Jesus tells them they must repent. If they fail to repent, if they continue to tolerate sin and heretical teachings, then he will make a decision: He will treat their hidden health problem with a scalpel. He calls that scalpel "the sword of my mouth" (Revelation 2:16).

Jesus says, "Repent therefore! Otherwise, I will soon come to you and will fight against them with the sword of my mouth" (Revelation 2:16). There is only one acceptable remedy. The remedy is not rationalizing sin, or psychoanalyzing the sin, or explaining why the sinners can't help themselves. No, the only remedy is *repentance.*

Choices have consequences. Jesus said the choice not to repent would result in a predictable outcome. The outcome is that the Great Physician's scalpel would penetrate deep into their lives.

Why? Because Jesus will *not* permit sin and false teaching to infect and infiltrate his bride. He will *not* allow cancer to grow in his body.

As the apostle Paul warned, "Do you show contempt for

the riches of his kindness, forbearance and patience, not realizing that God's kindness is intended to lead you to repentance?" (Romans 2:4). We must never take God's patience for granted. We should never mistake his kindness for tolerance of sin.

Jesus concludes his letter to the church in Pergamum with these words: "Whoever has ears, let them hear what the Spirit says to the churches. To the one who is victorious, I will give some of the hidden manna. I will also give that person a white stone with a new name written on it, known only to the one who receives it" (Revelation 2:17).

To those victorious believers who repent and turn to him, Jesus will give two rewards—hidden manna and a white stone with a new name written on it.

The hidden manna refers to the jar of manna that was preserved in the Ark of the Covenant. It is a reminder of God's grace in redeeming Israel from enslavement in Egypt.

But the real manna that comes from heaven is Jesus himself, as he told a crowd of followers during his earthly life. Someone in the crowd asked, "What sign then will you give that we may see it and believe you? What will you do? Our ancestors ate the manna in the wilderness; as it is written: 'He gave them bread from heaven to eat'" (John 6:30-31).

Jesus replied, "Very truly I tell you, it is not Moses who has given you the bread from heaven, but it is my Father who gives you the true bread from heaven. . . . I am the bread of life. Whoever comes to me will never go hungry, and whoever believes in me will never be thirsty" (John 6:32, 35).

When we truly, sincerely repent, we receive nothing less than Jesus himself.

Repentance also brings the reward of a white stone with a new name written on it. In the ancient world, a white stone was like an athletic trophy. Every victorious athlete received a white stone at the end of the competition, and their name was written on it. What does that mean?

When God called someone and set that person apart for a special purpose, he often changed their name. God called Abram and renamed him Abraham. God called Sarai and renamed her Sarah. God called Jacob and renamed him Israel. Jesus called Simon and renamed him Peter. Jesus called Saul and renamed him Paul.

God has a new spiritual name for you when you repent and lean on his strength alone. He gives you a new name and a new victorious identity. That name is engraved on the heart of every believer whose cornerstone is the Lord Jesus himself.

A LETTER TO
THE CHURCH OF JEZEBEL
Thyatira

Yuval Noah Harari, senior advisor to the World Economic Forum and a history professor at the Hebrew University of Jerusalem, has called for the Bible and other religious texts to be replaced by a "new Bible" written by artificial intelligence (AI). The purpose of a new machine-created "Bible" would be to invent a new global religion that reflects the World Economic Forum's progressive vision of worldwide "equity" and "inclusion."

As an atheist, Harari believes the Bible is a purely human creation, not inspired by God. "Throughout history, religions dreamt about having a book written by a superhuman intelligence, by a nonhuman entity. . . . In a few years, there might be religions that are actually correct. . . . Just think about a religion whose holy book is written by an AI. That could be a reality in a few years."[1] In other words, we could soon have a global religion based on a "Bible" written by the "superhuman intelligence" of AI.

Harari admits that the idea of a religion spawned by artificial intelligence has huge risks. "For thousands of years," he said, "prophets and poets and politicians have used language and storytelling in order to manipulate and to control people and to reshape society. . . . Now AI is likely to be able to do it. . . . It doesn't need to send killer robots to shoot us. It can get humans to pull the trigger. . . . We need to act quickly before AI gets out of our control."[2]

Harari has also promoted the idea that humanity can and should be replaced by artificial intelligence. "We just don't need the vast majority of the population" in the world today. People have become largely "redundant," and AI will "make it possible to replace the people."[3]

If that doesn't send a chill up your spine, I don't know what will.

As we edge closer and closer to the events described in the book of Revelation, we in the church need discernment and wisdom. The world is changing quickly—and an artificial intelligence–designed religion may be just around the corner. My guess is that such a religion would include enough reasonable-sounding Christianity to make it palatable to unwary Christians (but without the Cross and Resurrection, of course), plus generous portions of other religions to make this new AI-generated religion "equitable" and "inclusive" for everyone around the world.

It would be the perfect religion with which to elevate the Antichrist to power. And as we are about to see, it would not be the first time that people have tried to dilute and contaminate Christianity with pleasant-sounding falsehood and error. As we come to our examination of the first-century church in Thyatira, we are reminded of our desperate, urgent need for discernment and wisdom in the twenty-first-century church.

The Theme Is Discernment

The smallest of the seven cities in Revelation 2–3, Thyatira was located about forty miles southeast of Pergamum, where the modern Turkish city of Akhisar stands today. Thyatira was known for its thriving textile manufacturing and commerce. It was home to many guilds and trade associations and was famous for its production of a highly prized purple dye—the color of nobility and royalty.

The letter from the resurrected and glorified Jesus to the church at Thyatira is the longest of the Lord's seven letters to seven churches. Along with the letter to the Laodiceans, I think this is one of the most timely and relevant letters for the church today. Let's hear what Jesus said to the church at Thyatira.

To the angel of the church in Thyatira write:

These are the words of the Son of God, whose eyes are like blazing fire and whose feet are like burnished bronze. I know your deeds, your love and faith, your service and perseverance, and that you are now doing more than you did at first.

Nevertheless, I have this against you: You tolerate that woman Jezebel, who calls herself a prophet. By her teaching she misleads my servants into sexual immorality and the eating of food sacrificed to idols. I have given her time to repent of her immorality, but she is unwilling. So I will cast her on a bed of suffering, and I will make those who commit adultery with her suffer intensely, unless they repent of her ways. I will strike her children dead. Then all the churches will know that I am he who searches hearts and minds, and I will repay each of you according to your deeds.

Now I say to the rest of you in Thyatira, to you who do not hold to her teaching and have not learned Satan's so-called deep secrets, "I will not impose any other burden on you, except to hold on to what you have until I come."

To the one who is victorious and does my will to the end, I will give authority over the nations—that one "will rule them with an iron scepter and will dash them to pieces like pottery"—just as I have

received authority from my Father. I will also give
that one the morning star. Whoever has ears, let
them hear what the Spirit says to the churches.
REVELATION 2:18-29

The theme of this letter to Thyatira is discernment. I once
heard the concept of discernment illustrated with a story
that went like this: A young man in China wanted to learn
everything there is to know about jade, the "imperial gem."
He wanted to learn how to select the best varieties and colors,
how to carve it, how to polish it, and all the lore and history
of this beautiful stone. He went to an older man who was
reputed to be among the greatest experts on jade.

On the first day they met, the older man placed a small
jade stone in the young man's hand. "Hold on to that jade,"
the expert said. Then he proceeded to talk at length. He
lectured for hour after hour about philosophy and history—
but he didn't say a word about jade. At the end of their time
together, the older man asked the younger man to hand him
the jade stone.

On the second day they met, the older man again handed
the younger man a small jade stone, then lectured for hours
about philosophy and history. But the whole time they were
together, he said nary a word about jade.

The third day went exactly like the first and second.

And so did the fourth day.

And the fifth.

The young man was patient and polite on the outside,

but inwardly he was becoming frustrated. He thought, *I came here for one purpose—to learn about jade. This old man drones on and on about everything* but *jade! When will this old man teach me what I came here to learn?*

On the sixth day, the young man decided it was time to confront the older man and demand that he share his knowledge about jade. The two men sat down, and the older man handed the younger man a stone, as was their ritual.

The young man opened his mouth to voice his complaint—but then he stared at the stone in his hand. It looked like jade, it had the color and luster of jade, but it didn't feel right.

"This isn't really jade!" the young man said. "It's fake!"

"Now you are learning," the expert said.

Day after day, unbeknownst to the young man, the nerve endings in his hand were learning the weight and texture of real jade. Without realizing it, he was absorbing a valuable first lesson in his chosen craft: He had learned to discern between the genuine article and a fake.

Leaving a Legacy of Discernment

If I could go back and become a parent of little children again, I would spend more of my parenting time teaching discernment. If I could go back to the beginning of my years as a pastor, teacher, and author, I would spend more time majoring on the subject of discernment. The greatest legacy we can leave our children, our students, our congregation, the people we lead in the business world, the lives we touch in our neighborhoods—aside from the legacy of the gospel itself—is a legacy of modeling and teaching Christian discernment.

What does *discernment* mean? It is not merely a matter of distinguishing right from wrong. It is not merely a matter of distinguishing truth from falsehood. It is not merely a matter of distinguishing the primary from the secondary, the urgent from the trivial, the essential from the nonessential, the necessary from the superfluous, the best from the merely good, or the eternal from the transitory.

Discernment includes *all* those things, but it is much *more* than that.

Discernment is the all-important ability to remain anchored in the truth, anchored in reality, anchored in godliness and righteousness. It is the ability to avoid drowning in a sea of confusion. It is the ability to prevent ourselves from suffering a calamity of consequences arising from unwise and undiscerning choices.

The cost of going through life without discernment is a price no one can afford to pay.

In his letter to the church in Thyatira, Jesus points out that this church is undergoing a crisis of discernment. He begins with affirmation: "I know your deeds, your love and faith, your service and perseverance, and that you are now doing more than you did at first" (Revelation 2:19). This church was faithful to Jesus and was not ashamed to identify with him. They did not deny the faith. In fact, they practiced their faith with acts of service and perseverance. They probably fed and housed the poor and homeless. They gave generously to the needy. They put their faith and love into action.

But Jesus goes on to say, "Nevertheless, I have this against you: You tolerate that woman Jezebel, who calls herself a prophet. By her teaching she misleads my servants into sexual immorality and the eating of food sacrificed to idols" (Revelation 2:20).

We Have Come Full Circle

The patron god of Thyatira was Apollo, the Greek and Roman god who represented oracles, archery, knowledge, music and the arts, herds and flocks, and protection of the young. Thyatira, remember, was home to many guilds and trade associations—which we would know as trade unions today. These organizations had enormous power over the lives of the citizens of the city, and they were strongly associated with the worship of Apollo.

To have a job and earn a living in Thyatira, one had to be a member of a guild. Leather workers, dye workers, bronze workers, iron workers—each trade had its own guild, and each guild had a patron god. The guilds required their members to worship the patron gods at pagan festivals, which were held regularly. Those who attended the festivals were required to eat the meat that was offered to the guild's patron god—and the ceremony of sacrifice required the participants to engage in acts of sexual immorality.

So Christians in Thyatira faced a dilemma: In order to work and put food on the table for their families, they had to belong to a pagan guild and engage in pagan practices. What was a Christian to do?

The answer, according to one prominent false teacher in the church at Thyatira, a woman that Jesus calls Jezebel, was to go along to get along. She said, in effect, "You have to work, so go ahead and take part in these pagan festivals. While you're at the festival, eating meat sacrificed to idols and engaging in sexual immorality, you can witness to the pagans about your faith in Christ. You can live like a pagan during the week, then go to church like a Christian on Sunday."

When Jesus says, "You tolerate that woman Jezebel," a woman who leads Christians astray, he is essentially saying, "You lack discernment. You have lost your ability to distinguish right from wrong, truth from error. You have allowed immorality to infiltrate your faith and your church."

It is unlikely there was a woman in the church at Thyatira whose name was actually Jezebel. For Jews—and the church was largely Jewish at that time—it was a dishonorable and disreputable name, dating back the evil Queen Jezebel in 1 and 2 Kings. No Jewish parents would name their daughter Jezebel. Most likely, the term *Jezebel* describes a woman who had an unofficial leadership position in the church. Many churches have de facto "church bosses," who don't hold an official position but who are influential and intimidating. By calling this woman "Jezebel," Jesus was able to make a clear statement about her character—and he identified her in such a way that all the believers in Thyatira would have known who he was talking about.

The original Jezebel, in the Old Testament, was a wicked, non-Jewish, Syrophoenician woman, the daughter of the king of Tyre, a pagan kingdom. She married Ahab, a wicked king of Israel, as recorded in 1 Kings 16:30-31: "Ahab son of Omri did more evil in the eyes of the LORD than any of those before him. . . . He also married Jezebel, daughter of Ethbaal king of the Sidonians, and began to serve Baal and worship him."

Jezebel lived during the time of the prophet Elijah. You may recall that Elijah called down fire from Heaven that destroyed the prophets of Baal who had served Queen Jezebel. After a lifetime of unimaginable sin and wickedness, Queen Jezebel met her well-deserved end, being thrown out of a window by her own servants, where she was trampled in the streets by horses and her flesh was eaten by dogs (2 Kings 9:30-37).

Jesus compares the false teacher in Thyatira to this incredibly wicked woman in the Old Testament—a woman who led the people of Israel into error and sin. Just as the Old Testament Jezebel seduced Israel into Baal worship, so this New Testament Jezebel was seducing the believers in Thyatira into sin and idol worship. Many of the believers heard this advice from her and thought, "Hmm, I guess that makes sense. And she's very influential in the church, so she must know what is right and what is wrong. If she says it's okay for

A LETTER TO THE CHURCH OF JEZEBEL

me to compromise with idol worship and immorality, then it must be okay."

The church in Thyatira faced its greatest threat not from the pagans, not from a hostile government or a hostile Jewish community, but from a false teacher *inside* the church. And the errors of the first-century church are being repeated in the twenty-first-century church. After two thousand years, what's old is new again. We have come full circle to a perilous place where lack of discernment meets false teaching.

Jezebel in First-Century Thyatira

Jesus goes on to say of the Jezebel in the church at Thyatira, "I have given her time to repent of her immorality, but she is unwilling. So I will cast her on a bed of suffering, and I will make those who commit adultery with her suffer intensely, unless they repent of her ways. I will strike her children dead. Then all the churches will know that I am he who searches hearts and minds, and I will repay each of you according to your deeds" (Revelation 2:21-23).

The Lord's judgment against the Jezebel in Thyatira was supposed to stand as a lesson and a warning for all churches in all places at all times down through history. But we, in our day, seem to have forgotten that lesson and that warning. False teaching is as rampant today as it was in Thyatira—if not more so.

In the first century, one of the most prevalent heresies

105

to afflict and infiltrate the church was Gnosticism (from the Greek word *gnōstikos*, meaning "having knowledge"). Gnosticism was a collection of religious ideas that emphasized personal knowledge while rejecting Christian doctrine and the authority of the apostles. The Gnostics believed in a good but unknowable God of the mind and spirit, and a lesser and lower deity (called a *demiurge*) who created the inferior and corrupt material world. The Gnostics didn't believe in sin and repentance, but in illusion and enlightenment—and for them, "salvation" was merely a matter of attaining secret knowledge.

We don't know if the Jezebel of Thyatira was a follower of Gnosticism, but her false teachings do have a resonance of Gnostic dualism—the dualism between matter and spirit. This Jezebel seemed to be teaching the believers in Thyatira a false notion that goes something like this: "God is only interested in the spirit, not the body; so what you do with your body doesn't matter. If you want to eat food sacrificed to idols or engage in immoral acts—go ahead! You can do whatever you want with your body."

This Jezebel might have flattered the believers, praising them for their exemplary lives, for their deeds of love, faith, service, and perseverance. This would make it easier for her to plant this dualistic view of spirit versus matter in their minds and convince them it was perfectly compatible with the Christian faith. Then she could lure them into anything, even idolatry and immorality.

Jezebel in the Church Today

Features of this ancient heresy can be found in false notions that still infect the church in the twenty-first-century. We still see elements of this ancient, Gnostic dualism, the division between the material and the spiritual—a dualism that says, "God is only interested in the spirit. As long as you don't renounce your Christian faith, you can do whatever you want with your body. As the saying goes, 'Your body, your choice.'"

There are churches today that downplay the Bible in favor of an emphasis on spiritual gifts, faith, supposed miracles and healings, and special messages and new doctrines received directly from God. One leader in this movement claims to receive "downloads" of new doctrines and previously hidden insight from God. These churches teach that the Bible is essentially a starting place for understanding God, but that *real* knowledge of God is found "off the map" (that is, outside the Bible). They claim this knowledge comes through direct revelation from the Holy Spirit. Because the leaders of these movements receive these supposed revelations, they become an elite and privileged class within these churches.

This is twenty-first-century Gnosticism, and it is heresy. The apostles fought exactly this kind of heresy throughout their ministries, as the following Scripture passages show.

See to it that no one takes you captive through
hollow and deceptive philosophy, which depends on

human tradition and the elemental spiritual forces of this world rather than on Christ.

COLOSSIANS 2:8

Timothy, guard what has been entrusted to your care. Turn away from godless chatter and the opposing ideas of what is falsely called knowledge, which some have professed and in so doing have departed from the faith.

I TIMOTHY 6:20-21

But there were also false prophets among the people, just as there will be false teachers among you. They will secretly introduce destructive heresies, even denying the sovereign Lord who bought them— bringing swift destruction on themselves. Many will follow their depraved conduct and will bring the way of truth into disrepute. In their greed these teachers will exploit you with fabricated stories. Their condemnation has long been hanging over them, and their destruction has not been sleeping.

2 PETER 2:1-3

Dear friends, do not believe every spirit, but test the spirits to see whether they are from God, because many false prophets have gone out into the world. This is how you can recognize the Spirit of God: Every spirit that acknowledges that Jesus Christ has

come in the flesh is from God, but every spirit that
does not acknowledge Jesus is not from God. This is
the spirit of the antichrist, which you have heard is
coming and even now is already in the world.

I JOHN 4:1-3

Another form of twenty-first-century Gnosticism in the
evangelical church today is a view that theologians call "antinomianism." It comes from two Greek words, *anti* and *nomos*,
meaning "against law," and it refers to the idea that "under
the gospel dispensation of grace, the moral law is of no use or
obligation because faith alone is necessary to salvation."[4] You
will not hear this exact term used in these churches, because
they usually won't admit they are advocating the breaking of
God's law. But that is, in fact, what they promote.

For example, they will suggest that Jesus is *one* way to God
but not the only way. They will tell you that sex outside of
marriage is all right as long as both partners are "committed"
to each other. They will say that what made sexual immorality wrong in the Old Testament was that it was linked to idol
worship, but Christians in immoral relationships today don't
worship idols—they're covered by grace. They will rationalize
divorce, saying it is justifiable if one partner feels unsatisfied
in the marriage or falls in love with someone else. And on
and on.

Churches that dispense cheap grace and preach a cheap-
ened gospel are heretical—full stop, end of story. They have
undermined the teachings of Jesus, the apostles, and the Bible

regarding how we should live. Once we abandon God's law, we have abandoned the only objective standard that exists for structuring healthy families, healthy churches, and healthy societies. The antinomianism in today's church has led to a twenty-first-century dualism in which Christianity is seen to have authority only over lofty spiritual matters but has no effect on how we live our daily lives, use our bodies, and conduct our most important relationships.

Tragically, Jezebel is alive and well in many churches today. We who uphold the uncompromised Word of God must constantly be on guard against the infiltration of modern "Jezebelism" in the church today.

Encouragement for Those Who Reject Jezebel

The Jezebel in Thyatira knows who she is and what she has done—and she knows what Jesus expects of her. As Jesus himself says, "I have given her time to repent of her immorality, but she is unwilling" (Revelation 2:21).

Jesus makes his conditions clear. He commands those who follow false teachers to repent. He does not merely suggest it, or recommend it, or give them the option to repent. No, he *commands* them to repent. He gives them the *opportunity* to repent, to change direction, to turn their backs on false teaching and immorality.

But if Jezebel and her followers ("her children") do not repent, he says, "I will cast her on a bed of suffering, and I will make those who commit adultery with her suffer intensely, unless they repent of her ways. I will strike her children dead" (Revelation 2:22-23).

Jesus goes on to offer a strong word of encouragement for the faithful believers in Thyatira, those Christians who have rejected the false teachings of Jezebel. He says, "Now I say to the rest of you in Thyatira, to you who do not hold to her teaching and have not learned Satan's so-called deep secrets, 'I will not impose any other burden on you, except to hold on to what you have until I come'" (Revelation 2:24-25).

Hold on! Stand firm! Cling to the truth! Keep on keeping on!

Then he goes on to give an amazing promise: "To the one who is victorious and does my will to the end, I will give authority over the nations—that one 'will rule them with an iron scepter and will dash them to pieces like pottery'—just as I have received authority from my Father. I will also give that one the morning star. Whoever has ears, let them hear what the Spirit says to the churches" (Revelation 2:26-29).

We often hear the president of the United States referred to as "the most powerful man on Earth." But being the president of one nation is small potatoes. Friend in Christ, as faithful believers, we will one day rule over nations! We will rule and reign with Christ.

We often become so discouraged, disheartened, and bogged down by the sins and sorrows and troubles of this world that we forget the awesome power and authority that Jesus will one day place in our hands. We look at our squabbling, inept political leaders and say, "What is so difficult about balancing the budget? About maintaining a secure national border? About treating everyone equally and justly? About protecting our communities from being overrun by criminals? If I were in charge of the government, I know what I would do."

Well, one day we will exercise exactly that kind of authority over nations. Jesus will give us the wisdom and the responsibility to enforce his righteousness in the world. We will possess his delegated authority.

But he will entrust us with that authority in the future only if we are faithful to him today. He says, clearly and unambiguously, that he will give that power to "the one who is victorious and does my will to the end."

Those who have followed the Jezebels of this age should not expect to receive such authority from Jesus. Again and again, Jesus told his followers that those who are faithful with little will be entrusted with much (see Matthew 25:21; Luke 16:10; 19:17).

Furthermore, he said, "I will also give that one the morning star." The Morning Star is Christ himself. This means that we will share in his glory. When you turn your back on the darkness of this world, you will receive the light of God's glory. When you give up Jezebel, you will receive Christ. When you resist the allure of Satan, you will receive the Morning Star. When you turn your back on sin and compromise, you will receive the glory of Jesus.

Seek discernment! Pray that God will fill you with the Holy Spirit, who will make you wise and discerning, so that you can always distinguish truth from falsehood, right from wrong. Discernment will keep you from falling for the false teachings of the Jezebels of this age. And faithfulness to God's Word will give you a share in his glory and authority over the nations.

A LETTER TO A DEAD CHURCH

Sardis

I was born in Egypt. As a boy growing up in a Christian home in the Middle East, I was taught by my parents that my reputation is one of my most prized possessions. That message was reinforced by my teachers and the surrounding culture. I learned that a good reputation is more valuable than money, power, or prestige—more valuable, in fact, than life itself. They told me that if I ever lost my reputation, I would lose everything.

When I began to travel in parts of Asia in the 1970s and 1980s, I discovered that Asian cultures took the notion of a good reputation to an even greater extreme. They call it "saving face." In China, this concept is called *mianzi* (面子),

and it is related to the Western concept of honor, dignity, or public image. *Mianzi* means "face," but it is not a face you can see in the mirror. It's a face you must *earn* by your behavior. It's a face you can lose through misbehavior.

I once heard a Chinese proverb that says, "As trees cannot exist without bark, men cannot live without a face." Your "face"—your honor and reputation—is essential to maintaining your place in society.

Over the years, however, I have observed that an obsession with one's outward reputation can easily lead to hypocrisy. It can lead to an unhealthy concern for external appearances at the expense of an internal reality. I have known people—and I'm sure you have, too—who have a public persona that is very different from who they are in private.

This is the trap the Pharisees fell into at the time of Christ. They were only concerned with their outward reputation and external appearance. As Jesus told them, "Woe to you, teachers of the law and Pharisees, you hypocrites! You clean the outside of the cup and dish, but inside they are full of greed and self-indulgence. Blind Pharisee! First clean the inside of the cup and dish, and then the outside also will be clean" (Matthew 23:25-26).

Jesus wants our inner character to match our external reputation. He wants us to be whole people, with integrity inside and out. He does not want a church filled with Jekyll-and-Hyde split personalities. As someone once said, "If you spend too much time polishing your reputation, your character will become tarnished."

The late economist John Kenneth Galbraith was said to have had an elevated sense of his own superiority. He told a story from the days when he was ambassador to India under President John F. Kennedy. The *New York Times* had just run a profile of Galbraith that described him as "arrogant." Over breakfast at the White House with President Kennedy, Galbraith fumed, "I don't see why they called me 'arrogant'!"

"I don't see why *not*," the president replied. "Everybody else does."[1]

Sometimes we are the very last ones to know what our reputation really is.

The theme of the Lord's letter to the church at Sardis is this: The only reputation you should be concerned about is your reputation with God. Don't worry about what the world thinks of you. Focus on what God thinks of you. What people think of you is a fleeting matter, like smoke in the wind. But what God thinks of you is eternal.

A Message of Rebuke

Jesus' letter to the church in Sardis is one of rebuke. Near the end of the letter, he has some encouraging words for a faithful remnant in Sardis. But unlike the other six letters, he cannot begin this message with a word of affirmation. He doesn't have a compliment or a word of praise for the church as a whole.

Why not?

It's because the church at Sardis was obsessed with its

worldly reputation. It was focused on what the world thought of it. The believers in Sardis were sitting on their blessed assurance and doing nothing of spiritual value.

The world applauded Sardis and said, "What a progressive church it is! What an open-minded and tolerant church it is! The pastor is such a great communicator!" But Jesus had a very different perspective on the church at Sardis:

To the angel of the church in Sardis write:

These are the words of him who holds the seven spirits of God and the seven stars. I know your deeds; you have a reputation of being alive, but you are dead. Wake up! Strengthen what remains and is about to die, for I have found your deeds unfinished in the sight of my God. Remember, therefore, what you have received and heard; hold it fast, and repent. But if you do not wake up, I will come like a thief, and you will not know at what time I will come to you.

Yet you have a few people in Sardis who have not soiled their clothes. They will walk with me, dressed in white, for they are worthy. The one who is victorious will, like them, be dressed in white. I will never blot out the name of that person from the book of life, but will acknowledge that name before my Father and his angels. Whoever has ears, let them hear what the Spirit says to the churches.

REVELATION 3:1-6

Sardis was located about thirty miles southeast of Thyatira. The city was founded at least 1,500 years before the time of Christ, and its origins are lost to history. Around seven centuries before the resurrected and glorified Jesus Christ sent this letter, the city of Sardis reached its pinnacle as one of the greatest and wealthiest cities of the ancient world.

At one time, Sardis was the capital of the ancient kingdom of Lydia. In around 547 BC, Cyrus the Great of Persia defeated King Croesus of Lydia and conquered Sardis. (This was eight or nine years before Cyrus released the Israelites from their Babylonian exile and allowed them to return home to Jerusalem.) Though Sardis was looted and burned to the ground, it was later rebuilt under the Persians.

In 334 BC, Sardis was attacked and captured again, this time by the Greeks under Alexander the Great. The new conqueror rebuilt the city as an outpost of the Empire of Greece. In 129 BC, Sardis passed into the control of the Roman Empire.

These historical facts all have a bearing on our understanding of the letter to the church in Sardis. Why? Because Jesus takes a famous cultural characteristic of Sardis, and he warns the Christians in that city against the pitfalls of adopting those cultural characteristics.

Every city has a unique culture. Chicago, Portland, Los Angeles, New Orleans, Atlanta, New York, and Boston are all American cities, yet each one has its own distinct culture. What unique cultural characteristics set Sardis apart from the other six cities that Jesus sent letters to?

The most striking cultural characteristic of Sardis was that its people had a reputation for laziness and complacency. They were content to rest on their past glories and their wealth. Because of their luxurious lifestyle, they were spoiled and soft. They were unwilling to do the hard work of defending themselves from foreign invaders, so they had been easy prey for the Persians, the Greeks, and finally the Romans.

G. Michael Hopf, in his novel *Those Who Remain*, succinctly summarizes historical cycles, based on Strauss–Howe generational theory: "Hard times create strong men. Strong men create good times. Good times create weak men. And, weak men create hard times."[2] The city of Sardis was populated by weak, lazy men, so they were experiencing a cycle of hard times.

The self-satisfied laziness of Sardis had seeped into the mindset of the Christian believers there. The Lord Jesus looked upon the believers in Sardis, and deeply grieved by what he saw there, he sent this letter of warning.

Admonition, Antidote, Assurance

In his letter, Jesus impresses three main points on the believers in Sardis—an *admonition*, an *antidote*, and an *assurance*. He *admonishes* them for relying on their false reputation. He gives them an *antidote* so they can be restored. And he gives *assurance* to the faithful remnant of believers that they will receive a reward for their devotion.

First, let's look at the Lord's *admonition*. He says, "These are the words of him who holds the seven spirits of God and the seven stars" (Revelation 3:1). What does he mean when he refers to himself as the one who "holds the seven spirits of God and the seven stars"?

As we have seen, the number seven symbolizes completion or perfection. Jesus is saying that his spirit—the Holy Spirit—has complete and perfect knowledge of every believer. People may misunderstand us. They may misjudge us. They may mistreat us. But Jesus knows us all, completely and perfectly. He has complete authority over every church and every believer. They belong to him. That's why only he is qualified to expose the spiritual deficiency and bankruptcy of any church.

Jesus goes on to say, "I know your deeds; you have a reputation of being alive, but you are dead" (Revelation 3:1). There are many churches like Sardis today—churches with a reputation for being active and alive, but they are zombie-like, going through the motions of life while being lifeless within.

There are many churches today that have a large attendance, a huge budget, involvement in social causes and cultural relevance, and an outstanding reputation in the community. Nonbelievers can visit those churches and be perfectly comfortable, knowing they will never be challenged by the gospel. Sinners can feel comfortable there, knowing they will never be called to repentance. There are outreaches to the poor, entertaining programs for children and youth, cultural and artistic and musical events for the community, but Jesus looks at those busy, active churches with outstanding reputations and he sees a spiritual graveyard.

The Lord taught me long ago how deceptive appearances can be. I have lived long enough to know how deadly it is when the world speaks well of you. As a pastor, when secular media figures praise you, it's the kiss of death. I am perfectly happy being hated and mocked by the ungodly forces of this dying world.

I once heard someone say, "The world has become so churchy, and the church has become so worldly that I can't tell the difference between them." That statement puzzled me at first, but then I realized it was true. The world has become "churchy." As people in our post-Christian society have drifted away from genuine Christianity, they have not become less religious. They have simply replaced religion with other pursuits—especially politics—and they have made those pursuits their substitute religion.

Ryan Burge, who teaches religion and politics at Eastern Illinois University, observes, "Our politics has become religion. It has a religious fervor to it now that it didn't have even twenty or thirty years ago."[3] Whether we are see ourselves as liberals or conservatives, whether we are registered as Democrat, Republican, Libertarian, Green, Peace and Freedom, or None of the Above, we need to guard against making a religion out of our political views.

My observation is that the secularists on the progressive left have replaced the doctrines and creeds of Christianity with dogmas of social justice, "equity," and intrusive Big

Government (a secular substitute for a providential God). The secular left has replaced Christian morality with the false morality of neo-Marxism, which divides the world into "victims" and "oppressors" (where the victim groups are always righteous, and the supposed oppressors are always evil). The secular left has defined its own "salvation" narrative, replacing salvation by grace through faith in Jesus Christ with "saving the world" through social justice and green agendas. The secular left has also replaced the end times prophecies of the Bible with dire predictions of a climate change Armageddon.

Yes, the world has become "churchy." But it's also true that the church has become worldly—so that it's hard to tell the difference between the world and the church. Far too many churches have become Sardis-like, seeking the approval of the pagan culture. They use the world's techniques to create an entertainment experience instead of a worship and evangelism experience. They water down the demands of the gospel and dispense cheap grace.

Jesus gazes at these churches with his all-searching eyes, and he says to them (as he said to the church in Sardis so long ago), "You can't fool me or hide from me. I see straight through you. I know what is going on inside of you. I know your motives. I know your inward secrets. You have the reputation of being alive and vibrant, but I know better."

During the Lord's earthly ministry, Jesus repeatedly exposed the hypocrisy of the scribes and Pharisees. Here, in Revelation 3, he exposes the hypocrisy of the church in Sardis—and many churches in the twenty-first century.

The Antidote

We've looked at the Lord's admonition to the church at Sardis. Next, we will look at his antidote for the dead condition of that church.

Jesus says, "Wake up! Strengthen what remains and is about to die, for I have found your deeds unfinished in the sight of my God. Remember, therefore, what you have received and heard; hold it fast, and repent. But if you do not wake up, I will come like a thief, and you will not know at what time I will come to you" (Revelation 3:2-3).

His antidote is a literal wake-up call. The church in Sardis is like a smoldering campfire. Once it blazed brightly, but now it is nothing but dull red coals that are about to go cold. Jesus says there is still a spark left, there is still a residue of heat that can be fanned into a flame.

But for the fire to spring up once more, the believers in Sardis must *wake up* and recognize their pathetic spiritual condition. They must *wake up* and return to the truth of the gospel. They must *wake up* and pray for those whose hearts for God have become cold, dead cinders.

Do you recognize yourself or your church in the Lord's description of Sardis? Then wake up and repent! Now is the time to grieve over your true spiritual condition. When Christians repent, the church comes to life. That is the phenomenon we call *revival*.

A colleague of mine in the United Kingdom sent me information about the great wave of revival that began in

Wales and the Hebrides Islands in 1904. It was the largest Christian revival in Wales during the twentieth century—so large that it quickly spread to other countries. Across Wales, shops would close at midday for prayer. Churches were filled with praying people twenty-four hours a day. Men and women, boys and girls, with tears streaming down their faces, were praying over friends and family members who didn't follow Christ.

In the Welsh coal mines, the ponies that pulled the rail cars in the mines would not move because the coal miners had stopped cursing—and cursing was the only language the ponies knew. Broken marriages were restored. People repented of wrongs and made amends to those they had hurt. Major newspapers, such as the *Western Mail* and the *South Wales Daily News*, spread the news of great waves of conversions.

The revival spread across the Atlantic to America. Thousands of people gathered in major cities, praying to receive Christ and to be filled with the Holy Spirit. Newspapers in America published the names of new believers.

Upon hearing this historical account from my friend in the UK, I cried out to God and said, "Do it again, Lord!" Oh, that God would visit us again and awaken us! Oh, that he would deliver us from living on our reputation!

If Jesus has a message to churches in the twenty-first century, it is this: Don't be deceived by the size of your megachurch congregation, your megachurch budget, and your mega-toleration of sin and error. Don't confuse a large crowd with true revival. Don't confuse entertaining music and glib crowd-pleasing sermons with genuine worship and authentic biblical preaching. Wake up! Grieve over sin! Repent! Pray for revival!

That is the Lord's antidote for a sleeping, dying church like the one in ancient Sardis—and countless others today.

The Assurance

Even though the risen and glorified Lord Jesus had no word of affirmation for the Sardis church as a whole, he did have a word of assurance for a tiny faithful remnant there. In fact, he gives them a twofold promise.

"You have a few people in Sardis who have not soiled their clothes," Jesus says. "They will walk with me, dressed in white, for they are worthy. The one who is victorious will, like them, be dressed in white. I will never blot out the name of that person from the book of life, but will acknowledge that name before my Father and his angels. Whoever has ears, let them hear what the Spirit says to the churches" (Revelation 3:4-6).

The first promise is that the few faithful believers in Sardis will be clothed with white robes. In the Bible, a white robe is a symbol of both righteousness and of celebration and festivities. We know from the parable of the wedding banquet, in Matthew 22:1-14, that all followers of Jesus will be dressed in wedding robes for the wedding supper of the Lamb (see Revelation 19:6-9).

In the parable, when the rich and snobbish elites refuse to come to the wedding banquet for the king's son, the king invites people from the streets to come to the banquet—and they are fitted with wedding robes to show that they are invited guests. (The king, of course, represents God the Father, and the groom represents Jesus the Son.) One person sitting at the table is found to be without a wedding robe—and since he is not properly clothed, the servants cast him out of the wedding banquet and into the darkness outside.

Those who are invited to the wedding supper of the Lamb in Heaven will receive a white robe from Jesus—the Groom himself. White robes are also a symbol of victory and purity. Jesus will give a white robe to each believer who has remained pure and unstained by the filth and corruption of this world. He will give a white robe to every believer who wins the victory over temptation and sin.

Does Jesus mean that we must be perfect to receive a white robe? No. We can never achieve complete moral perfection in this life. But we must hate sin—and whenever we sin, we must have a heart that simply cannot wait to confess that sin and repent of it. When we confess our sin and ask for God's forgiveness, he will give us a white robe that covers our sin and blots it out of his sight. That robe is the righteousness of Jesus.

The white robe also stands for resurrection. We cannot earn eternal life with Jesus in Heaven. We cannot earn our resurrection from death. Eternal life is a gift of the Lord's grace, which he gives freely to all his faithful children.

But that's not all! Jesus also gives us a second promise: He assures us that our names are indelibly inscribed in the Book of Life: "I will never blot out the name of that person from the book of life, but will acknowledge that name before my Father and his angels" (Revelation 3:5).

This promise would have had a special meaning for the people of Sardis and other cities that had been under Greek and Roman rule. Those ancient cities maintained registries of citizenship—and Sardis, which was once the capital of the ancient kingdom of Lydia, was renowned for its royal archives, where they recorded a citizen's name, status, tax obligations, military service, and so forth. When a citizen committed a crime against the state, that person's name would be blotted from the registry—and then they would be executed.[4]

But Jesus assures us that he has recorded our names in the Book of Life in Heaven. It is written not in pencil, not even with pen and ink, but with the indelible and infinitely precious blood of Jesus. He wrote our names there so that no one could ever erase them, write over them, or blot them out.

One day, I will hear my name read from that book. When Jesus calls my name and acknowledges me before God the Father, I will fall to my face and say, "Thank you, Jesus! Thank you for saving me, redeeming me, sustaining me, and acknowledging me before the Father. I have acknowledged you before men. Now, true to your word, you have acknowledged me before the Father."

There's an old gospel song that says, "When the roll is

called up yonder, I'll be there." That song is about this very moment when our names will be read from the Book of Life. When the roll is called in Heaven, will you be there?

If you have any doubts about whether your name is written in the Book of Life, settle the matter right now. Go to Jesus and say, "I have nothing to offer you except my sin. I have no righteousness of my own. I freely confess my sin, I repent of it, and I need your forgiveness and grace. I surrender my life to you. Take control of my life. Teach me how to live for you, in grateful obedience, from this day forward."

The Bible tells us, "If you declare with your mouth, 'Jesus is Lord,' and believe in your heart that God raised him from the dead, you will be saved" (Romans 10:9). The moment you confess and believe, God will answer you from Heaven and your name will be inscribed forever in the Book of Life.

THE MOST JOYFUL LETTER
Philadelphia

Years ago, a friend told me about a conversation he'd had after giving a talk at a prayer breakfast for Christian business-people. The theme of his talk was "the tragedy of missed opportunities." Afterward, a man came up to him and said, "Thank you for speaking to our group—though, in a way, I'm sorry you gave us that message."

Puzzled, my friend said, "What do you mean, you're sorry I gave that message?"

"Well, when you talked about the tragedy of missed opportunities, you reminded me that I have missed God's best for my life—and it really makes me sad. There was a time, when I was younger, that I felt God calling me to become a missionary overseas; but I decided I knew best. I chose to devote my early years to making a lot of money, and I figured there would always be time later to go to the mission field. Well, I've made more money than I could spend in three lifetimes, but I regret the fact that I have missed out on God's best for my life."

My friend replied wisely, "In God's economy, it's never too late. I believe this with every ounce of my being. Start where you are now, pray for God's will for the rest of your life, and then go where he tells you to go and do what he tells you to do."

Do you live with regrets like that businessman? Do you feel you passed up opportunities God has placed in your path? It's not too late to turn to God and offer him the rest of your life. God's Word tells us from cover to cover that he is in the redemption business, the forgiveness business, and the restoration business.

In the book of Joel, God speaks to wayward Israel. The Jewish nation had turned its back on God's best, on God's will for the nation. So God called Israel to repent and seek forgiveness. He told Israel it was not too late—and he offered an abundance of blessings if Israel would respond and repent:

"Even now," declares the LORD,
    "return to me with all your heart,
    with fasting and weeping and mourning. . . .

"I will repay you for the years the locusts have eaten."
JOEL 2:12, 25

Isn't that a beautiful promise? If we turn to him, God will repay us for the years the locusts have eaten. Past opportunities may never be repeated, but if you say, "Lord, here I am. Use me now! Open any door and I'll walk through it," God will repay you for the wasted years and set you on the path of blessing.

In his letter to the believers in Philadelphia, our resurrected and glorified Lord points these faithful Christians to God's open doors of opportunity. Of all the seven letters Jesus sent to the seven churches, I think this is the most joyful and delightful letter. It is a letter that any faithful believer would love to receive from Jesus.

I'm sure that this letter brought indescribable joy to the hearts of the believers in the city of Philadelphia.

No Perfect Christians, No Perfect Churches

Our precious Lord was very pleased with the little struggling church in Philadelphia of Asia Minor. This small, persecuted church brought great joy to his heart. In the Lord's letter to the believers in Philadelphia, we do not find one word chastising them for tolerating sin or welcoming false teachings. If any church in the first century approached perfection, this was that church.

Now, I'm not saying that the Philadelphian believers were morally and spiritually perfect. No believer nor any church could ever achieve perfection in this life.

The great Bible teacher Charles Haddon Spurgeon (known

as the Prince of Preachers) made this clear in a sermon he preached in 1884. "Do you want to be perfect, and to join with perfect [people]?" he said. "If you do, do not come to this church, because I will warrant you there is not a perfect member in it, though there are many of the excellent of the earth in our midst. . . . We shall be very glad to receive you if you love the Lord and are prepared to obey his commands. That is all we require. . . . If you were to join a perfect church, I am sure it would not be perfect after you had been admitted into it. You had better give up that idea."[1]

As long as churches are made up of human beings, and until the day Jesus returns and we are all changed to become like him, there can be no such thing as a perfect church. Why? Because there is no such thing as a perfect Christian.

There can be such a thing as a faithful church, a biblically sound church, a Christ-centered church, an obedient church. But there is no perfect church.

The church in Philadelphia wasn't perfect, but it was faithful and obedient. The faithfulness of that little body of believers thrilled the heart of our Lord, as his letter makes clear:

To the angel of the church in Philadelphia write:

These are the words of him who is holy and true, who holds the key of David. What he opens no one can shut, and what he shuts no one can open. I know your deeds. See, I have placed before you an open door that no one can shut. I know that you have little strength, yet you have kept my word and have not denied my name. I will make those who are of the synagogue of Satan, who claim to be Jews though they are not, but are liars—I will make them come and fall down at your feet and acknowledge that I have loved you. Since you have kept my command to endure patiently, I will also keep you from the hour of trial that is going to come on the whole world to test the inhabitants of the earth.

I am coming soon. Hold on to what you have, so that no one will take your crown. The one who is victorious I will make a pillar in the temple of my God. Never again will they leave it. I will write on them the name of my God and the name of the city of my God, the new Jerusalem, which is coming down out of heaven from my God; and I will also write on them my new name. Whoever has ears, let them hear what the Spirit says to the churches.

REVELATION 3:7-13

There's no mistaking the tone of joy and delight that drenches this letter from the risen and glorified Lord Jesus to the faithful believers in Philadelphia.

An Open Door That No One Can Shut

The Greek city of Philadelphia was established in 189 BC by King Eumenes II of Pergamum, who named the city in honor of his brother and successor, Attalus II. Because Attalus was known for his great brotherly love for Eumenes, his nickname was Philadelphos, meaning "the man who loves his brother." The city was located in the fertile valley of the Cogamus River. The Ottoman Empire conquered Philadelphia in 1390 and renamed it Alaşehir, which is the modern name of this now-Turkish city.

At the time the book of Revelation was written, Philadelphia was home to many pagan temples. Today, the city of Alaşehir is home to dozens of Islamic mosques. Yet, throughout the history of this city, there has always been a faithful Christian remnant, and there are Orthodox and Roman Catholic churches in Alaşehir to this day.

Ancient Philadelphia was a crossroads of the ancient world. Situated on the Persian Royal Road, running between Sardis and the city of Susa, it was known as the Gateway to the East. The Greeks used Philadelphia as a springboard to propagate Greek culture, to promote the Greek language, and to spread the Greek way of life eastward into Asia Minor. Why were the Greeks so eager to influence the world?

At that time, the Greeks considered themselves more refined and sophisticated than the rest of the world. They were proud of their arts, their religion, and their philosophy. They saw themselves as culturally superior to the other peoples of the world, whom they viewed as barbarians.

Modesty ought to forbid me from saying this—but I'm going to say it anyway: The Greeks felt superior to everyone

THE MOST JOYFUL LETTER

else until they came to Egypt. Then they discovered what *real* culture and civilization looked like!

All kidding aside, we will see in this letter that Jesus takes the reputation of Philadelphia as the Gateway to the East and applies it to the church. He tells these believers, in effect, "Your city is known for being a springboard from which to export Greek culture and Greek language. Now I have a greater vision for you and a greater message for you to export. I am placing before you a message of life and death that you need to take to the rest of the world. I am placing before you an open door that no one can shut—a door of evangelism and witness to the entire world."

The believers in Philadelphia suffered persecution. They faced obstacles and opposition. They struggled with weaknesses and handicaps. If they wanted to make excuses, they had many problems and difficulties to choose from.

But making excuses was not in the Philadelphian character. They chose to remain faithful even in trying circumstances. They endured. They stood firm. The Lord was delighted with their courage and steadfastness.

And please do not miss this: The Lord's message that he is opening a door of opportunity for sharing the Good News is the very heart of this letter to the believers in Philadelphia: "See, I have placed before you an open door that no one can shut" (Revelation 3:8).

God always provides opportunities for us to share our faith. God always opens doors that no one can shut. God always provides us with people who have open hearts and

open eyes to hear the Good News of the gospel of Jesus
Christ. The question is, do we have the spiritual eyes to see
them? Do we have the spiritual sensitivity to recognize them?
Do we have the courage to seize the opportunities? Are we
willing to walk through the open doors?

Doors of Opportunity

Here's a fact that we all too easily forget: Doors of opportunity do not remain open forever. This is my own opinion,
not a statement from the Word of God, but based on my
observation of the political and social climate of the world
around us, I feel very strongly—and urgently—that we in
the West have a very narrow period of opportunity left to
share Christ openly, to proclaim the truth without fear, and
to exercise our freedom of speech and religion. This moment
of opportunity is fleeting and will disappear before long. The
world is changing quickly, and our freedoms are crumbling
so swiftly that it may be only a matter of *months*, not years,
before we lose it altogether.

I'm absolutely convinced that a time is coming quickly
when we will have to pay a price to proclaim biblical truth.
Your pastor may have to go to jail to stand firmly for God's
Word. You may lose your career or be expelled from your
school for daring to share Christ with a friend. Your witness
may lead to your arrest.

You may think I'm exaggerating. I'm convinced that I'm

not. I have given the coming persecution a lot of thought. I have calculated the cost. I'm prepared for whatever comes.

But in the meantime, the door of opportunity is still open. The Lord Jesus has placed before us an open door that no one can shut—no one, that is, but Jesus himself. And there will come a time when he says, "It's time to shut the door."

Right now, the door is open. We need to use that open door as a portal for urgent, vibrant witness—for as long as we can.

There are many places in the world where God's people are afraid to go to church. They have been threatened by their governments. They have been threatened by their neighbors. They still gather to worship Jesus and encourage one another—but they know they are risking their freedom and their lives. They are placing their families at risk.

If you live in America, you have enormous freedom—for now. You can invite your friends and neighbors to a ballgame, a movie, a party, a backyard barbecue—but do you ever invite them to church?

And what about your own church attendance? The New Testament reminds us that we should "not [give] up meeting together, as some are in the habit of doing, but [encourage] one another—and all the more as you see the Day approaching" (Hebrews 10:25). After the pandemic forced many people to "attend" church via YouTube or Zoom, at least until the COVID-19 virus subsided, many people got into the habit of staying home in their pajamas and sipping coffee and even playing games on their phones while listening with one ear to church on their computers.

My friend, that is not attending church and it is not pleasing to the Lord. Of course, if you are a shut-in who is physically unable to attend church, you know that I'm not referring to you. But there are many people who *can* attend church, who know they *should* attend church, but they don't. We need to be physically present with other believers, encouraging them and receiving encouragement from them.

The local church is a rallying point, a place where we gather as one to get our spirits stirred so that we can go out, advance into the world, and take territory for Jesus and his Kingdom. The time is now. The opportunity is here. The door is open.

But someday that door will shut. Soon your witness will be outlawed. Soon your freedom will be curtailed.

The Limits of God's Patience

You may wonder why the door might remain open for only a limited time. Answer: Because Jesus holds the only master key to this door. When the day comes that we lose our freedom of speech and our religious liberty and our freedom to proclaim the gospel, it will be because Jesus himself has shut the door.

Remember what he said: "These are the words of him who is holy and true, who holds the key of David. What he opens no one can shut, and what he shuts no one can open" (Revelation 3:7).

When the door closes, it will not be the government that closes it. Nor will it be the political left or right, nor will it be the Democrats or Republicans or even the Communists. It will not be the militant atheists. It will not be the secularists. One of those groups may be the instrument Jesus uses to shut the door, but no one can thwart his will or force his hand. Jesus is the sovereign Lord of history. Nothing happens that he does not permit.

You might ask, "Why would Jesus shut the door?"

The answer: God is patient with his children, but his patience is limited. His timetable may be long, but it is not infinitely long. It must eventually come to an end.

Jesus is saying, in effect, "I have opened the door and only I can shut the door. Now is the time to serve me. Now is the time for obedience. Now is the time for witness. Now is the time to expand the Kingdom. Now is the time to gather together and worship in freedom. A time will come when the door will be shut; it will be dangerous and illegal to witness and to worship. Seize this present opportunity while you still can."

Don't harden your heart to the opportunity of this present moment, because the opportunity may not come again. In the book of Exodus, Moses told Pharaoh to let God's people go. But Pharaoh hardened his heart and would not obey God. And when a person hardens their heart, God says, "Very well, if that's what you want, you can have it—and I'll give you more of what you want. If you wish to harden your heart, all right, I'll harden it even more."

That is why, after Pharaoh first hardened his own heart,

we read, "But the LORD hardened Pharaoh's heart and he would not listen to Moses and Aaron, just as the LORD had said to Moses" (Exodus 9:12). If you harden your own heart toward God, he may harden it more.

I urge you: Do not delay. Do not procrastinate. Do not harden your heart. Seize this present opportunity and walk through the door while Jesus holds it open.

Storming Satan's Stronghold

Years after America was attacked by terrorists on September 11, 2001, President George W. Bush said we "must continue . . . to take the fight to our enemies across the world."[2] He understood that, to have victory, we cannot just be on the defensive. We must go on the offensive. The same principle applies in spiritual warfare.

Many Christians are spiritually hunkered in the bunker, complaining, "I'm under attack by Satan." They're too paralyzed by fear to take territory for the Kingdom.

But Jesus calls us to leave the bunker and storm Satan's strongholds. Jesus is the one with all authority in Heaven and on Earth—and he commands us to go on the offensive and invade Satan's citadels in the name of Jesus. He calls us to claim Satan's territory in the name of the Lord.

As we take Satan's strongholds, we will rescue the perishing, heal the wounded, and bind up the brokenhearted. We will set the captives free in the name of Jesus.

But we do not have much time left. The enemies of the

Cross are plotting, planning, and strategizing—and they are deceiving weak Christians. Instead of teaching believers how to be discerning, how to increase their faith, how to witness with boldness, we are fighting with each other over silly, unimportant matters. And Satan is loving it!

Soon the door will be shut. Soon the opportunity will disappear. The era of freedom and favor we now enjoy will come to an end.

Now is not time to sit in a defensive crouch, with our head in our hands, waiting for the end to come. This is a time for decisive action. This is a time for bold witness. Ask God for courage and wisdom—and then win souls and take territory for Jesus.

Three Obstacles and a Threefold Promise

The resurrected and glorified Lord Jesus identifies three major obstacles the church in Philadelphia faced, and he gives them a threefold promise. The three major obstacles the believers faced were *a lack of strength*, *persecution by religious zealots*, and *a coming hour of trial*.

1. *A lack of strength.* He says, "I know that you have little strength, yet you have kept my word and have not denied my name" (Revelation 3:8). The church in Philadelphia was friendless. The people had no political power or allies. They didn't participate in the pagan cultural and religious rituals, so they were social outcasts. They had no one in the

community or the government to support them or protect them from persecution. As a group, these believers were weak and vulnerable to the point of powerlessness.

2. *Persecution by religious zealots.* Like the believers in Smyrna, the believers in Philadelphia were being slandered by "the synagogue of Satan, who claim to be Jews though they are not, but are liars" (Revelation 3:9). Again, when the Lord refers to "a synagogue of Satan," he doesn't mean these people worship the devil, but they have been duped by the devil into doing his bidding. They are deeply religious Jews who are zealous for God, but they spread lies concocted by Satan.

Satan wants to silence Christians any way he can. If he can't destroy a believer, he will try to paralyze that believer with fear. And he often uses persecution to instill fear in the Christian community.

3. *A coming hour of trial.* Jesus calls this threat "the hour of trial that is going to come on the whole world to test the inhabitants of the earth" (Revelation 3:10).

The resurrected and glorified Lord Jesus counters these three obstacles with a threefold promise. If believers will walk through the door he has opened, if they will shake off their reluctance and move out in bold obedience, he will *vindicate* them, *protect* them, and give them *a new identity.* And here's a crucial feature of these three promises: Each one begins with the words "I will."

1. *Jesus promises vindication.* "I will make those who are of the synagogue of Satan, who claim to be Jews though they are not, but are liars—I will make them come and fall down at your feet and acknowledge that I have loved you" (Revelation 3:9). The enemies of the believers, the ones who are now slandering them and reporting them to the authorities, will have to eat their words. Like it or not, they will fall at the feet of the believers. They will publicly acknowledge that the followers of Christ were truly doing the will of God.

2. *Jesus promises protection.* "I will also keep you from the hour of trial that is going to come on the whole world to test the inhabitants of the earth" (Revelation 3:10). The foundations of the world will one day be shaken, but Jesus will keep his people safe from the hour of trial and destruction. Do you worry about the terrors of the last days? Do you fear for yourself, your family, your children, your grandchildren in that time of testing?

Make sure you have prepared them by sharing the gospel with them. Make sure your own salvation is assured. Then trust Jesus. He has promised that if we are faithful to him, if we have placed our trust in him, if we have walked through that open door in obedience to his will, we have nothing to fear during "the hour of trial." He will ensure our eternal safety and protection.

Jesus goes on to say, "I am coming soon. Hold on to what you have, so that no one will take your crown. The one who is victorious I will make a pillar in the temple of my God.

Never again will they leave it" (Revelation 3:11-12). Why does Jesus use the symbol of a pillar? Why does he portray believers as pillars in the temple of God?

A pillar suggests stability and strength. A pillar is permanent and immovable. If you visit the ancient ruins of the Greek temples in these seven cities, you will not see very many roofs or walls, but you will see many, many pillars. The pillars once supported massive stone structures, which have long since crumbled—but the pillars still stand.

The pillars in those ruins were constructed to honor certain pagan deities. But the believers in Philadelphia will be pillars in the temple of God. They will not be flimsy, temporary signposts. They will be permanent, strong, immovable columns that stand forever in honor and praise to God.

There may be another reason Jesus chose the symbol of a pillar to symbolize these believers. Throughout its history, the city of Philadelphia was often rocked by earthquakes. Perhaps it is this geological instability and peril of Philadelphia that prompted the Lord Jesus to promise the believers there that they would become a symbol of rock-solid stability.

3. *Jesus promises a new identity.* "I will write on them the name of my God and the name of the city of my God, the new Jerusalem, which is coming down out of heaven from my God; and I will also write on them my new name. Whoever has ears, let them hear what the Spirit says to the churches" (Revelation 3:12-13).

Jesus assured the persecuted believers in Philadelphia that

he would give them a new name, a new identity. Here again, Jesus was probably referring to the history of the city of Philadelphia. Twice in the first century AD, Philadelphia was renamed. During the reign of the Roman emperors Caligula and Claudius, the city was called Neocaesarea (New Caesar City). Later, after Emperor Vespasian founded the Flavian dynasty, Philadelphia was known for about a decade as Flavia Philadelphia in honor of the new imperial house.

The city of Philadelphia changed its name to honor different emperors. Similarly, Jesus has promised to give his people a new name to honor King Jesus. That is our identity. That is who we are. We are citizens of the eternal Kingdom of Heaven, which is ruled by our Lord and Savior, King Jesus.

Our Eternal Destination Is Rising

Apollo 8 was the first manned spacecraft to orbit the moon. The crew—Frank Borman, James Lovell Jr., and William Anders—lifted off from planet Earth on December 21, 1968. They orbited the moon ten times without landing, then returned safely to Earth, splashing down on December 27, six days after departure. The three *Apollo 8* astronauts were the first human beings to see the far side of the moon, which always faces away from Earth.

If you think there isn't much to do aboard a spaceship on the way to the moon, you'd be very mistaken. The *Apollo 8* astronauts were intensely busy most of the time with tasks of life-and-death importance.

Navigator Jim Lovell was occupied with taking star sightings using a sextant to determine the spacecraft's exact location—but his job was made especially difficult by a debris cloud around the spacecraft that obscured his view of the stars. Meanwhile, the other crew members, Frank Borman and William Anders, were struggling to keep the spacecraft turning on its axis once an hour—a "barbecue roll" designed to evenly distribute the heat of the sun across the skin of the vehicle. The spacecraft was prone to wobbling instead of spinning, so the astronauts had to make frequent adjustments with the attitude jets. They knew that if the spacecraft's skin got too hot or too cold, fuel lines could explode, or the heat shield could crack—and they would all die.

The crew ran into additional problems when they tried to fire the course correction engine, which turned out to be underpowered. When it was time for Borman to take his turn sleeping, he found that the constant radio chatter and mechanical noises gave him insomnia. He took a sleeping pill—but the pill made him feel nauseated and caused him to vomit. This meant that the crew had to spend precious time cleaning up a mess that floated in the cabin.

As *Apollo 8* approached the moon, several windows fogged up, obscuring the astronauts' view of the lunar surface. And because of the rotation of the spacecraft and the need to constantly monitor instruments, the crew had little time for moon gazing.[3]

On the third day of the mission, Christmas Eve 1968, *Apollo 8* was on the far side of the moon. William Anders pointed his Hasselblad 500 EL camera through a window, taking pictures of the lunar surface. Suddenly, he shouted, "Look at that picture over there! There's the Earth coming up. Wow, that's pretty!"[4]

The other astronauts crowded around Anders. Together, those three men became the first human beings to see the Earth rising from behind the moon. The sight took their breath away. The photo snapped by William Anders in that moment became one of the most reprinted pictures ever taken: *Earthrise*, the image that revealed to the world the fragile beauty of our little planet as it floats through the blackness of space.

The next day—Christmas Day—the three astronauts made a live television broadcast back to Earth. Each crewman gave his impression of the lunar landscape below them. Then they took turns reading the biblical Creation story from Genesis 1. Borman ended the broadcast by wishing everyone, "Good night, good luck, a Merry Christmas and God bless all of you—all of you on the good Earth."[5]

Later that day, the spacecraft began its journey home.

The story of *Apollo 8* reminds me of the story of our lives. We face stresses, problems, and obstacles every day—many of which seem of life-or-death importance at the time. We easily become so focused on our problems, so preoccupied with the urgencies and emergencies of daily life, that we forget to look up toward the face of God.

Those astronauts were struggling to survive in space, struggling to keep their little spacecraft rotating safely in space—until the moment their home planet came into view. Their first glimpse of planet Earth, rising above the curved horizon of the moon, changed everything. It gave meaning to their mission. It turned a mere journey around the moon into a spiritual pilgrimage. It enabled them to read from the first chapter of the Bible and reflect on the wonder of the existence of God and his universe.

I urge you in the name of Jesus—do not become too preoccupied with the urgent and the temporary. Do not become so obsessed with problems, crises, and details that you leave no room for gazing upon the face of God, for contemplating your origin and your destination.

Just as Earth rose above the curvature of the moon, our eternal destination is rising before us. Seize every opportunity to serve Jesus. Invest every moment in loving and worshiping him. Right now, he holds the door open—a door that only he can shut.

Step through the door. Give your life to him. Let him take you on the adventure of a lifetime.

A LETTER TO
A LUKEWARM CHURCH
Laodicea

Do you follow extreme sports?

I don't, but I'm fascinated by the fact that there are athletes who seem addicted to a high degree of physical risk. These athletes seem to crave the adrenaline rush that comes with extreme speed, height, depth, difficulty—and yes, extreme danger.

Extreme sports are the mainstay of The X Games and the Extreme Sports Channel, and they include such thrill-and-stunt sports as skateboarding, skiing, snowboarding, snowmobiling, surfing, wakeboarding, off-road motorcycle racing (motocross), bicycle motocross (BMX), skydiving,

BASE jumping (BASE stands for *building, antenna, span,* and *earth*), and more. Here's a short list of athletes who have died in pursuit of that adrenaline rush.

Malik Joyeux was known as a happy big-wave surfer from Tahiti who warned kids not to use drugs. In 2005, Joyeux was surfing the famous Oahu Pipeline in Hawaii when a massive wave crashed on him, destroying his board and drowning him. He was twenty-five.

Jimmy Hall was famed for swimming with man-eating sharks in Hawaii—but it wasn't a shark that killed him. In 2007, Hall was BASE jumping from three-thousand-foot vertical cliffs on Canada's Baffin Island when he mistimed his parachute deployment and crashed into the mountainside. He was forty-one.

Caleb Moore was known for doing amazing stunts on snowmobiles. During the 2013 Winter X Games, he attempted an aerial jump with a backflip, but he landed with the snowmobile on top of him. The impact damaged his heart. He walked away from the crash, but collapsed, dying a few days later at age twenty-five.

Erik Roner was a German skydiver who died performing what should have been an easy parachute jump. In California in 2015, he performed a stunt with two other parachutists for a celebrity golf tournament. He slammed into a tree and died at age thirty-nine.

Uli Emanuele was a wingsuit jumper. While live-streaming a daring jump in the Italian Dolomite mountains in 2016, he crashed and died. He was twenty-nine.[1]

Clearly, the life of an extreme sports athlete is a dangerous life. I certainly don't want to tell other people how to live their lives. But for me, the thrill of careening at breakneck speeds or somersaulting through the air or diving through a canyon like a flying squirrel doesn't seem worth the risk of my one-and-only irreplaceable life.

And yet I'm convinced that most of those who sit in front of their screens watching extreme sports are at far greater risk than the extreme athletes they are watching. After all, who is in greater danger, the athlete who has practiced and calculated and carefully planned each feat, or the couch-potato spectator, gobbling down artery-clogging snack foods? Who is at greater risk, the athlete who is fanatical about fitness or the spectator who has accepted his fatness?

Despite the danger of extreme sports, I think the athlete is in less danger than the spectator. The athlete has a stronger heart, greater lung capacity, better circulation, a lower stress level, and better prospects for a long life than the junk food junkie.

Spiritual Couch Potatoes

Are you wondering what sort of spiritual application I could possibly make from this comparison? Well, it is simply this: God wants his people to be extreme athletes for his Kingdom. He wants us to be willing to go to extremes for the gospel. He wants us to be willing to take risks—not foolish gambles, not throwing our lives away without thinking, but meaningful, calculated, purposeful risks to advance his Kingdom around the world.

The great tragedy of the church in the twenty-first century is that it is made up largely of spectators and consumers instead of participants and risk-takers. Far too many Christians—who should be giving, serving, ministering, and doing—are spiritually lazy. They want to be safe, secure, and entertained, so they never take risks for Jesus.

The result is that these spiritual couch potatoes have become unhealthy. Their love for Jesus is weak. They have poor spiritual circulation. Their spiritual lungs wheeze instead of inhaling grace and exhaling the Good News of Jesus Christ. Their hearts do not beat for the things that warm the heart of Jesus. The next crisis or shock in life might tip them into spiritual cardiac arrest. They are on their way to a spiritual demise.

And that's the kind of believer Jesus is speaking to in his letter to the church at Laodicea.

To the angel of the church in Laodicea write:

These are the words of the Amen, the faithful and true witness, the ruler of God's creation. I know your deeds, that you are neither cold nor hot. I wish you were either one or the other! So, because you are lukewarm—neither hot nor cold—I am about to spit you out of my mouth. You say, "I am rich; I have acquired wealth and do not need a thing." But you do not realize that you are wretched, pitiful, poor, blind and naked. I counsel you to buy from me gold refined in the fire, so you can become rich; and white clothes to wear, so you can cover your shameful nakedness; and salve to put on your eyes, so you can see.

Those whom I love I rebuke and discipline. So be earnest and repent. Here I am! I stand at the door and knock. If anyone hears my voice and opens the door, I will come in and eat with that person, and they with me.

To the one who is victorious, I will give the right to sit with me on my throne, just as I was victorious and sat down with my Father on his throne. Whoever has ears, let them hear what the Spirit says to the churches.

REVELATION 3:14-22

The Laodicean church, like so many churches today, was breaking the heart of Jesus. They had the distinction of being the only church about whom the risen and glorified Lord Jesus had *nothing* good to say.

Some Bible scholars claim that these seven churches represent seven periods or ages of time, and that we are now in the Laodicean age. I disagree with this view. I believe all seven letters were written to all churches and all believers in every place and for all times.

But whether you agree with me or not doesn't matter.

However you interpret these letters, I think you'll find that the letter to the Laodicean believers applies to every church today. Along with the letter to the church at Thyatira, this is one of the most urgently needed letters for the church in the twenty-first century.

A City of Worldly Success

Laodicea was located on a hill overlooking the Lycus River, near where the modern Turkish city of Denizli stands today. It was founded by Antiochus II, king of the Seleucid Empire, sometime between 261 and 253 BC. He named the city in honor of his wife Laodice. Located on a major trade route, Laodicea was one of the wealthiest cities of the ancient world. The city also had a large population of Jews, whom Antiochus had brought from Babylon. Many of these Jews later became Christians through the ministry of the apostle Paul.

Paul apparently wrote a letter to the Laodicean church that has been lost to history. In Colossians 4:16, Paul tells the Christians at Colossae, "After this letter has been read to you, see that it is also read in the church of the Laodiceans and that you in turn read the letter from Laodicea."

The finest clothing in the region was manufactured from rich, glossy wool from the sheep that grazed on the hills outside the city. The city was home to many pagan temples and monuments, two theaters, a stadium, baths, a gymnasium, government buildings, a medical school, and even a mint that produced Laodicean coins.

Laodicea stood as a model of worldly success. If business consultants had been plying their trade in the first century, they would have begun every PowerPoint presentation by saying, "Let me tell you about Laodicea." It was the center of finance and business in the region. Every investment and brokerage firm in the region would have to have an office—if not headquarters—in Laodicea. It was a city of luxury and conspicuous consumption.

Even some Christians in Laodicea partook of the wealth of the city and were living the good life. But Jesus was not impressed by the wealth of the Laodicean Christian community. To paraphrase his words to them, "You may be the financial capital of the world, but you live in grinding spiritual poverty. You may be the clothing capital of the world, but you should be ashamed of your spiritual nakedness. You may boast of the eye salve that your medical center produces, but you are spiritually blind."

Neither Cold Nor Hot

In most of the seven letters of Revelation 2–3, the resurrected and glorified Lord Jesus applied a characteristic of the city to the church in that city. In his letter to the Laodiceans, Jesus refers to the city's water supply.

Some cities in the region had refreshing cold springs, while others had bubbling, steaming hot springs. But Laodicea had its water piped in from a great distance. Most cities of the Roman empire that had to import water used open aqueducts—channels that conveyed water by simple gravity. But because Laodicea sat on a hill, the water was conveyed through a pressurized pipeline, so that it went downhill into the valley, then up the hill. The water that reached the city was tepid and full of minerals and impurities. The stone pipes became encrusted, and even choked, by these impurities.

The water of Laodicea was not hot enough to relax in like the hot mineral baths in nearby Hierapolis. Nor was it cold and refreshing to drink, like the streams of nearby Colossae. Laodicea had a reputation in the region for its horrible water—water that was neither hot nor cold. It wouldn't poison you, but it was unpleasant to drink. In fact, people with stomach ailments were encouraged to drink large amounts of Laodicean water because it would induce vomiting.

So Jesus compared the Laodicean church to the Laodicean water: "These are the words of the Amen, the faithful and true witness, the ruler of God's creation. I know your deeds, that you are neither cold nor hot. I wish you were either one or the other! So, because you are lukewarm—neither hot nor cold—I am about to spit you out of my mouth" (Revelation 3:14-16).

Jesus was saying to them, "You are like your water. Your indifference and complacency make me sick. Your apathy nauseates me. Your halfhearted commitment is like a glass of your water—it makes me want to vomit."

As one Bible teacher has said, "Some churches make the Lord weep. Others make Him angry. The Laodicean church made Him sick."[2] Those words undoubtedly describe many churches in the world today.

The Cure Jesus Offers

What is the cure when a church—or an individual believer—is neither cold nor hot, but nauseatingly lukewarm? Jesus gives the believers in Laodicea the answer in three parts:

1. He alerts them to their fatal condition.
2. He counsels them to turn away from their fatal condition.
3. He promises that he will reward those who turn back to him.

The warning

First, Jesus alerts the Laodicean believers to the danger they are in. He says, "You say, 'I am rich; I have acquired wealth and do not need a thing.' But you do not realize that you are wretched, pitiful, poor, blind and naked" (Revelation 3:17).

We all have our blind spots—some worse than others. That's why we need to go before the Lord daily, asking him to show us our faults and sins so that we can grow to become more like Jesus. That's why we need fellow Christians to hold up a spiritual mirror to us and reflect back to us the reality of who we are.

When God or a fellow believer points out one of your character flaws, how do you react? Do you say, "Thank you for pointing that out. I didn't see that, and I'm really glad I have you in my life to illuminate my blind spots"? If that is your reaction, you are a rarity in the human race!

Most people, when confronted with a sin or flaw, react with annoyance, irritation, or outright anger: "How dare you criticize me! Who do you think you are? You've got some pretty annoying character flaws of your own, you know!"

Those are two possible reactions to having our blind spots pointed out: gracious acceptance or angry denial. But there's a third reaction that I sometimes see. I call it the "apathetic response." You point out an apathetic person's blind spots, and they just shrug and say, "So?"

If you tell this person, "Your blind spot is your apathy," they will likely shrug and say, "I'm not in favor of apathy— but I'm not against it either."

I believe apathy is the number one enemy in a believer's life. Why? Because apathetic people make terrible disciples. Apathetic Christians make Jesus sick.

During his earthly ministry, Jesus had twelve disciples. Each of the Twelve was a distinct individual with his own unique personality traits, strengths, and flaws.

There were some disciples who were too *hot*, such as Simon Peter and Simon the Zealot. Peter was impulsive and headstrong, and Jesus had to teach him to show more stability and humility. Simon the Zealot was a hotheaded activist against Roman rule, and Jesus had to teach him that God's Kingdom is spiritual, not political. Jesus was successful in helping these two hotheads learn to simmer down.

Jesus also had disciples who were too *cold*, such as Philip and Thomas. In John 6:5-7, Jesus tested Philip by asking him how they would feed a large crowd. Philip responded with doubt and reluctance instead of faith. When Jesus proceeded to feed five thousand people, starting with a few bread loaves and some dried fish, he was teaching Philip to "turn up the heat" on his cold, hesitant faith.

Thomas was known for his skepticism, his cautious nature, and his pessimistic temperament—all *cold* qualities. When Jesus told the disciples he was going to die in Jerusalem, Thomas gloomily said, "Let us also go, that we may die with him" (John 11:16). After the Resurrection, "Doubting Thomas" was the last disciple to accept the truth that Jesus had risen from the dead—and Jesus had to confront Thomas's cold nature and light a fire under his faith.

Jesus was able to cool down his hotheaded disciples, and he was able to fire up the disciples whose faith was too cold. But Jesus can't do very much with a tepid, lukewarm, apathetic person. Such people just make him sick.

In his letter to the believers in Laodicea, our risen and glorified Lord Jesus tells them, in effect, "You may be materially rich, but you are spiritually penniless. Your wealth has made you smug and self-satisfied. You are resting on your worldly reputation. Your faith is in material possessions, not in me. You are conceited and complacent and blind to your true condition. You dress in designer clothes, but you are spiritually naked."

All sins are infectious, but the sin of pride is the most

infectious and dangerous sin of all. That's why Jesus spoke so bluntly to the Laodiceans about their pride and complacency. Pride had infected the entire church in that city, so Jesus had to sound an urgent alarm and alert the Laodicean Christians to the spiritual danger they were in.

The counsel

Next, Jesus pleads with the Laodicean believers to turn away from their fatal condition. He says, "I counsel you to buy from me gold refined in the fire, so you can become rich; and white clothes to wear, so you can cover your shameful nakedness; and salve to put on your eyes, so you can see" (Revelation 3:18).

Notice those three words: "*I counsel you.*" They send chills up my spine. The God who said, "Let there be light" and summoned the stars and galaxies into existence is the same God who says to you and me, "I counsel you."

Jesus could have said, "I order you!" or "I command you!" or "I demand of you!" But no, he firmly but gently gives us advice and counsel—and it's up to us to wisely heed his counsel or ignore it at our own peril. He respects the freedom he's given us.

When I see a person foolishly, disobediently causing harm to other people—harm they don't seem to see—I want to pray, "Lord, stop them! Make them change their mind! Knock some sense into them."

But God says, "Mind your own business. I am already

counseling that person. I'm appealing to them in my own patient way."

God has the power to terrify us—but he will not. God has the power to run roughshod over our free will—but he will not. He prefers to counsel us, to appeal to us, to guide us, to lead us.

Yes, there are dire consequences if we ignore his counsel. There's a price to pay for stubborn disobedience. But God always begins by counseling us. And when he counsels us, we need to listen and respond. We must not close our ears and harden our hearts to his counsel, because a day will come when we will no longer be able to hear his voice.

When I was six years old, my father built a new house in a new part of town, not far from the railroad tracks. It was a beautiful house, and I looked forward to moving into it. Finally, the day came, and we took possession of our new house.

The first night I slept in that house, I was awakened by the scream of a train whistle. I must have jumped a foot off the bed! I thought the train was going to roar right through my bedroom. I had a hard time getting back to sleep after that unnerving experience.

The second night, it happened again. The train whistle woke me up, but I wasn't frightened, and I quickly got back to sleep.

The third night, the train whistle awakened me, but I instantly fell asleep again.

After a week, the whistle didn't even wake me up anymore. I was used to it. I slept through the nightly train whistle because I could no longer hear it.

The same principle applies to the counsel of God. When we hear him speaking to us, we need to respond immediately, while it is still loud enough to wake us up from our apathy. Do not ignore the voice of his counsel. When he speaks, do not roll over and go back to sleep—or else a time will come when you won't be able to hear his voice anymore, and then it will be too late. You will suffer the consequences of rejecting God's counsel.

The promise

Finally, Jesus promises that he will reward those who heed his counsel and turn back to him. His counsel is to buy from him gold refined in the fire so we can become rich; white clothes to wear so we can cover our shameful nakedness; and salve for our eyes so we can see.

What does Jesus mean when he tells us to come and buy from him? Obviously, he is not saying that we can buy our salvation. After all, salvation is a free gift that Jesus himself purchased with his own blood. So, what does he want us to buy? Answer: Jesus offers us nothing less than the greatest bargain in the history of the universe. He is saying, in effect, "Come in repentance and I will exchange your sin and failure for my forgiveness and healing. Come and I will exchange your pride and your sin for my humility. Come and I will exchange your worthless self-righteousness for my true righteousness. Come and I will exchange the rust and corruption of your stubbornness and rebellion for the authentic gold of obedience."

Only a foolish person would turn down that bargain.

My wife will tell you I'm a bargain hunter. I refuse to pay full price for anything. I know a good deal when I see one. I can assure you that what Jesus offers us is the bargain of a lifetime.

Let's be absolutely clear: Jesus isn't offering to exchange items that are equivalent in value. No, he is offering to accept our trash and give us his riches. He is offering to accept our sin and give us his forgiveness. He is offering to accept our worries and give us his peace.

You probably noticed that this letter contains one of the most famous verses in the Bible, a verse that is often quoted as a salvation appeal: "Here I am! I stand at the door and knock. If anyone hears my voice and opens the door, I will come in and eat with that person, and they with me" (Revelation 3:20).

You may wonder: Were the believers in Laodicea merely lukewarm Christians, or were they not believers at all? Was Jesus appealing to them to fire up a faith they had been neglecting? Or was he appealing to them to receive him as Lord and Savior for the very first time?

If Satan has blinded someone's heart, it doesn't matter whether that person is a backslidden and apathetic believer or a total unbeliever. It doesn't matter whether that person has turned his back on the truth or if he has never heard the truth. The message of Jesus to the apathetic believer and the total unbeliever is the same: "I stand at the door and knock. If anyone hears my voice and opens the door, I will come in."

Consider this amazing truth: Jesus is the Master of the house. He *owns* the place. But does he beat down the door and force his way in? No. His knock is gentle. His presence is respectful. He is giving people an opportunity to respond freely and gratefully.

He will not force his way in. He will wait patiently outside the door, and he will keep knocking. But when his time of waiting has ended, there will be no more patience, no more knocking—because it will be Judgment Day.

And don't miss this detail: Jesus doesn't merely invite us to breakfast. Nor does he say, "Let's do lunch." No! He says he will come in and have a long, satisfying, *intimate* meal with us. English translations, unfortunately, fail to capture the real meaning of this verse.

The NIV says, "I will come in and eat with that person, and they with me." The Greek verb translated here as "eat" appears only four times in the New Testament, with two of the occurrences being in the context of the intensely intimate Last Supper (see Luke 22:20; 1 Corinthians 11:25).

In the ancient world, people shared their big meal, their intimate meal, in the evening. This was the time when everyone shared their thoughts and experiences of the day. This intimate meal was the foundation of the fellowship of the family. And that is the meal Jesus promises to eat with us and share with us if we invite him into our lives.

Will you open the door of your heart to him? Will you respond to his patient knocking?

Jesus has alerted us to our condition, he counsels us to turn to him, and he rewards those who respond to him. His greatest reward is this: "To the one who is victorious, I will give the right to sit with me on my throne, just as I was victorious and sat down with my Father on his throne" (Revelation 3:21).

Imagine that!

Prince Philip, the Duke of Edinburgh (1921–2021), was the husband of Queen Elizabeth II. Queen Elizabeth loved her husband, but he was officially the queen's consort, not the king of England, so he was not allowed to share the throne.

Yet Jesus will let us reign with him on his throne! This reward exceeds all other promises that Jesus makes in the other six letters to the churches. It exceeds them all in glory. It exceeds them all in honor. It exceeds them all in authority.

Jesus says to the Laodiceans—and to us—"Let me into the chambers of your heart. Invite me into the control room of your will. Then I will take you into my Father's throne room, where all the great decisions that affect the universe are made."

He is saying, in effect, "Hand me the authority over everything that is important in your life, and I will give you the authority to run the universe with me." What an amazing bargain!

Do You Have Ears to Hear?

Jesus concludes his letter to the Laodiceans the same way he concludes the other six letters: "Whoever has ears, let them hear what the Spirit says to the churches" (Revelation 3:22). I didn't comment on that statement in the preceding six chapters, but I will explain it here.

When Jesus says, "Whoever has ears, let them hear," he is saying that we should not read these seven letters and think about all the *other* people these words apply to. We must not read these seven letters and think, "This person or that person really needs to read this and take it to heart! This church or that church really needs to heed the Lord's words and shape up!"

No, "Whoever has ears, let them hear" means, "This message is for *you*, not somebody else. You must listen to it. You must heed it. You must apply it. You must put it into practice. Not someone else. *You.*"

Every admonition in these seven letters was meant for you and me—*personally*. Every promise in these seven letters was meant for you and me—*specifically*. Every encouragement in these seven letters was meant for you and me—*individually*. Do you have ears to hear? Then apply these messages in your own life today.

These seven messages are meant not only for believers, not only for unbelievers, not only for members of churches, not only for people who lived in the ancient world, not only for people who live in the twenty-first century. They are meant for anyone and everyone who has ears to hear.

Whatever message you need to hear is in these seven letters.

If you need to be warned, then heed the warning of the Lord!

If you need encouragement, then bask in the thrilling promises of the Lord!

If you are apathetic, then allow the Lord's words to fire you up with enthusiasm!

If you are a Christian couch potato, get off your duff and get in the game!

If you have ears to hear, then listen to what Jesus says to you—and do it!

RECLAIMING OUR TRUE IDENTITY IN CHRIST

Alan Shlemon is an author and speaker for the Christian organization Stand to Reason. He recalls attending a missions conference where a missionary was going to talk about how to share the gospel with Muslims. The missionary said, "I never ask a Muslim to become a Christian. That's because Muslims can enter the Kingdom of God *as Muslims*, and still remain Muslim."

"I looked around me," Shlemon recalled, "wondering if I was in a church or a mosque. I waited for a gasp from the audience, but none came, not even a murmur. . . . No one seemed to note anything amiss. Except for me."[1]

The heretical and unbiblical view that horrified Alan Shlemon is called the Insider Movement. Tragically, it is steadily gaining acceptance among many pastors and missionaries. It has spread like a pandemic of heresy through many churches. The Insider Movement teaches that a Buddhist can follow Jesus while remaining a Buddhist, a Hindu can follow Jesus while remaining a Hindu, and so forth.

In many cases, the Insider Movement has led to a blending of Christian and non-Christian beliefs—a syncretism (merging or blending) of incompatible beliefs that is sheer apostasy. Those who try to syncretize Christianity with another religion may call themselves Buddhist-Christians or Hindu-Christians. Some adherents to Christianity-plus-Islam have even given their heretical mash-up the name *Chrislam*.

But Muslim doctrines, which deny the atoning death and resurrection of Jesus, simply cannot be reconciled with faith in Christ. The Buddhist worldview cannot be merged with faith in Christ. The many gods of Hinduism cannot be blended with faith in Christ.

Tragically, some in the church are willing to dilute the demands of the gospel. They have so weakened Christian doctrine that we now find ourselves surrounded by all sorts of "hyphenated Christians"—Gay-Christians, Trans-Christians, LGBTQ-Christians, Deconstructed-Christians, Universalist-Christians, Progressive-Christians, and on and on. They want to give every political, ethnic, cultural, and sexual identity its own gospel.

A New Identity

Jesus didn't die on the cross to give each so-called *identity* its own gospel. He died to give each believer a *new* identity—in *him*. There should be no hyphenated Christians in the church of Jesus Christ. That's why God's Word tells us, "There is no difference between Jew and Gentile—the same Lord is Lord of all and richly blesses all who call on him" (Romans 10:12). We are all one in Christ, and he is not divided, nor is he hyphenated.

If I may use myself as an example, I don't call myself a hyphenated American, even though I was born in Egypt and became an American by choice. Once I became an American citizen, I proudly adopted *American* as my sole national identity. In the same way, I believe a Christian, a citizen of the Kingdom of Heaven, should have an unhyphenated identity.

My identity as a Christian is simple: I am a redeemed child of God. I am on my way to Heaven. My sins are paid for, my redemption has been purchased by the blood of Jesus, and I am eternally forgiven. I once was lost but now I'm found. That is my identity and I need no other.

That is what Revelation 2–3 is all about. These two chapters, containing the Lord's seven letters to seven churches of the early Christian era, deal again and again with our identity in Christ.

Those seven churches all faced challenges and persecution. Some of those churches were success stories, some were failures. Some earned the Lord's praise, but five received stinging rebukes for their toleration of falsehood and sin.

If Jesus were writing a letter to the twenty-first-century church, I'm sure he would once again rebuke the church's tolerance of error and false doctrine. He would rebuke the church's tolerance of sin and immorality. He would rebuke the church's attempt to water down God's justice and judgment. He would call for repentance from a path of soft-pedaling Hell and promoting the unbiblical and un-Christian notion of universalism.

The toleration of sin and error in the church today stems from the twenty-first-century church's waning love for Jesus and increasing love for the world. The theorizers and academics of the church can claim all they want that they are simply trying to make the gospel "relevant" in the internet age. They can justify it as a new approach to witnessing for Christ.

But it all comes down to this: Their love for the world has overcome their love for Jesus. Their desire to be approved by the world has overcome their desire to be approved by the Master.

The Compromised Bride

The church is the bride of Christ—but the bride has begun to drift away from her husband. Her affections have begun to wander. She is still married to Jesus. She is still living with her loving husband, but she's no longer madly in love with him.

As the bride of Christ, we may have started with great love for Jesus. But after seeing how the world hates Jesus and his church, after hearing our moral standards condemned by the world as "narrow-minded" and "bigoted"—we have begun to waver in our affection for him. The easy path of compromise now seems appealing to us. We no longer witness at work, in the neighborhood, or on campus.

To win the approval of the world, we have begun to erase the distinctions between ourselves and our corrupt and dying world. We have begun to talk like the world. We have begun to love the things the world loves. We are no longer distinctly Christian. We have become *compromised, disaffected, worldly.*

We still attend church. We still sing songs about Jesus. We still have our favorite Bible passages. But we no longer seek to challenge the unconverted or confront sinners. We no longer preach the uncompromised Word of God. Our love for Jesus has become words on paper. We no longer live to honor, obey, and please Jesus alone. The world has caught our eye and divided our affection.

The temptation to stray from Jesus and compromise his truth has plagued the church from its inception. That's why Jesus appeared to John on the isle of Patmos and gave him the startling panoramic vision we know as the book of Revelation. That is why John preserved for us these seven letters to seven churches, straight from the lips of Jesus himself.

Again and again in these letters, we have seen that if we truly desire to remain in love with Jesus, we must deliberately, unapologetically, unwaveringly refuse to compromise with the culture. We must become a force of stubbornly counter-culture Christians.

Once we *compromise* with the culture, once we *accommodate* the culture, once we seek the *acceptance* and *approval* of the culture, we will lose our vision of what it means to be a Christian. We will lose our distinct identity as Christians. We will lose the power and force of our witness for Christ.

It takes courage and faith to stand firmly for Jesus and against the culture. As we saw in chapter 1, we live in a post-Christian age and persecution against Christians is increasing. I believe Satan is behind the growing persecution of Christians today. He is stoking hatred in human hearts. He is taking out his rage against believers. Satan hates God and he hates God's people, so he is provoking violence and oppression because he knows his time is short.

This is no time to drop our guard. This is no time to relax our spiritual vigilance. When I look at events around the world, I am reminded of the words found in four places in the Old Testament: "'Peace, peace,' they say, when there is no peace" (see Jeremiah 6:14; 8:11; Ezekiel 13:10, 16). Jeremiah was warning Israel of coming destruction, but false prophets were telling the people to ignore Jeremiah. "Peace is coming! Everything's going to be just fine."

I hear many voices today that sound a lot like those false prophets. I don't believe peace is coming. I believe trouble is headed our way—and we need to be ready.

That's why we need to study these seven letters from Revelation, and we need to obey the warnings and admonitions of our Lord. As Paul told Timothy, "Preach the word; be prepared in season and out of season; correct, rebuke and encourage—with great patience and careful instruction. For the time will come when people will not put up with sound doctrine. Instead, to suit their own desires, they will gather around them a great number of teachers to say what their itching ears want to hear" (2 Timothy 4:2-3).

What Is Your Patmos?

Sometimes in these pages, I have given you my opinion, which I have clearly marked as such. But as I close this book, I want to tell you on the authority of the Word of God that, no matter what you are going through right now, no matter what trials you are suffering, no matter how much persecution and mocking you must endure right now, no matter how deep your grief may be—nothing can ever separate you from the love of God in Jesus Christ (Romans 8:35-39).

In the first chapter of Revelation, John writes, "I, John, your brother and companion in the suffering and kingdom and patient endurance that are ours in Jesus, was on the island of Patmos because of the word of God and the testimony of Jesus." In other words, John had been exiled to the island of Patmos as a punishment because he preached the Word of God and taught the gospel of Jesus Christ.

But was he discouraged? No! He goes on to say that, while he was on Patmos, he was "in the Spirit" (Revelation 1:10). It didn't matter to John that he was far from home, separated from his family and Christian friends. His location made no difference, because he was in the Spirit. God was present with him wherever he went, even into exile on a lonely Roman outpost.

You may be on your own Island of Patmos right now. You may feel you have been exiled by persecution at work or school, by the loss of a loved one, by cancer or some other illness, by financial woes, by rebellious children or a difficult marriage, or by feelings of failure and disillusionment. Whatever your Patmos may be, you feel confused and frustrated, and you're probably saying, "Lord, why am I stuck in this situation? Why am I exiled here?"

The only way to overcome your Patmos experience is the same way John overcame his: Live in the power of the Spirit of God. Live in reliance on the Spirit of God. John endured his exile because he was in the Spirit. And so will you.

Remember, if John had not been exiled on the island of Patmos by the oppressive Roman government, if he had not been punished by Emperor Domitian for his faithful teaching of the gospel of Jesus Christ, the book of Revelation might not have been written. It may well be that John had to leave Ephesus and suffer isolation on Patmos for Jesus to break through and reveal to him this stunning apocalyptic vision.

Whatever you are going through, please remember that God can use you wherever you are. Your time of exile could be your time of greatest blessing and effectiveness. God revealed the mystery of the ages to John during his exile on the island of Patmos. What great mystery is he about to reveal to you?

Notes

INTRODUCTION: AN URGENT MESSAGE FOR OUR TIME

1. Open Doors, "World Watch List 2024," OpenDoors.org, 2024, https://www.opendoors.org/en-US/persecution/countries/.
2. Brett McCracken, "Why We Don't See Church as 'Essential,'" The Gospel Coalition, May 22, 2020, https://www.thegospelcoalition.org/article/church-essential/.
3. Alec Schemmel, "'No Legitimate Basis': Biden Admin Blasted for Directive Telling FBI to Investigate Parents at School Board Meetings," 3LV News (Las Vegas), The National Desk, March 22, 2023, https://news3lv.com/news/nation-world/no-legitimate-basis-judiciary-committee-blasts-biden-admin-directive-telling-fbi-to-investigate-school-board-meetings; Katy Grimes, "CA Education Board Approves 'Pornographic' Sex Ed," May 9, 2019, https://californiaglobe.com/fr/ca-education-board-approves-pornographic-sex-ed/; Joel Davidson, "School Board Silences Anchorage Dad for Objecting to Anal Sex Book in Student Libraries," *Alaska Watchman*, February 8, 2023, https://alaskawatchman.com/2023/02/08/school-board-silences-anchorage-dad-for-objecting-to-anal-sex-book-in-childrens-libraries/.
4. "Little Sisters of the Poor v. Commonwealth of Pennsylvania," The Becket Fund, accessed April 8, 2024, https://www.becketlaw.org/case/commonwealth-pennsylvania-v-trump/.
5. Kathryn Taylor, "An 8th Grade Girl Explains Why Male Athletes Should Not Be Allowed in Women's Sports," Reality's Last Stand, March 30, 2023, https://www.realityslaststand.com/p/an-8th-grade-girl-explains

-why-male; California Family Council, "CA Student Confronts School Board for Allowing Allegedly Violent Male to Use Girls' Restroom," CaliforniaFamily.org, May 8, 2023, https://www.californiafamily.org /2023/05/ca-student-confronts-school-board-for-allowing-allegedly -violent-male-to-use-girls-restroom/.

6. William Wolfe, "Yes, Christians Are Being Persecuted in America. Here's How We Can Respond," The Standing for Freedom Center at Liberty University, July 12, 2022, https://www.standingforfreedom.com/2022/07 /yes-christians-are-being-persecuted-in-america-heres-how-we-can -respond/.

7. "Atlanta Paid $1.2 Million for Axing Christian Fire Chief," Alliance Defending Freedom, November 13, 2023, https://adflegal.org/article /atlanta-paid-12-million-axing-christian-fire-chief.

CHAPTER 1: WARNINGS AND ENCOURAGEMENT FROM JESUS

1. R. Babcock, J. O. Choules, and J. M. Peck, eds., *The Baptist Memorial and Monthly Record*, vol. IV, no 5 (New York: John R. Bigelow, 1845), 130.

2. Babcock, Choules, and Peck, *Baptist Memorial and Monthly Record* 129, 131-132. (A man named Bartlett Bennett was present and transcribed Patrick Henry's speech. Italics in original.)

3. Emily Belz, "Pro-Life Protestor Acquitted in Federal Case," *Christianity Today*, January 30, 2023, https://www.christianitytoday.com/news/2022 /october/charges-prolife-protestors-abortion-clinics-dobbs.html; Emily Belz, "Federal Convictions of Pro-Lifers Blocking Clinics Are Rising," *Christianity Today*, February 2, 2024, https://www.christianitytoday.com /news/2024/february/abortion-clinic-prolife-protestors-convicted.html; Joe Bukuras, "Acquitted Pro-Life Activist Mark Houck Reveals Details of 'Reckless' FBI Raid; Will Press Charges," Catholic News Agency, February 1, 2023, https://www.catholicnewsagency.com/news/253523 /acquitted-pro-life-activist-mark-houck-reveals-details-of-fbi-raid-will -press-charges.

4. "Partnerships Established with NAACP, the National Urban League, and the Southern Poverty Law Center," Federal Bureau of Investigation press release, FBI.gov, April 27, 2007, https://archives.fbi.gov/archives/news /pressrel/press-releases/partnerships-established-with-naacp-the-national -urban-league-and-the-southern-poverty-law-center.

5. Bob Moser, "The Reckoning of Morris Dees and the Southern Poverty Law Center," *The New Yorker*, March 21, 2019, https://www.newyorker .com/news/news-desk/the-reckoning-of-morris-dees-and-the-southern -poverty-law-center; Tyler O'Neil, "Another Left-Wing Smear Campaign,"

The Heritage Foundation, March 7, 2023, https://www.heritage.org
/religious-liberty/commentary/another-left-wing-smear-campaign.
6. Jeff Johnston, "SPLC Continues to Label Conservative Christian
Organizations as 'Hate Groups,'" *Daily Citizen*, March 9, 2022, https://
dailycitizen.focusonthefamily.com/splc-continues-to-label-conservative
-christian-organizations-as-hate-groups/.
7. Paul Bedard, "Southern Poverty Law Center Website Triggered FRC
Shooting," *Washington Examiner*, February 6, 2013, https://www
.washingtonexaminer.com/?p=1579914.
8. John Clark, "Illinois Bill Proposes Charging Parents Denying Children
Abortion or Gender-Affirming Care with Child Abuse," MyStateLine.com,
February 22, 2024, https://www.mystateline.com/news/local-news/illinois
-bill-proposes-charging-parents-denying-children-abortion-or-gender
-affirming-care-with-child-abuse/; "Illinois Bill Would Target Parents If
Kids Denied Abortion or Gender Services," *Decision*, February 23, 2024,
https://decisionmagazine.com/illinois-bill-would-target-parents-if-kids
-denied-abortion-or-gender-services/.
9. Michael Dorstewitz, "New California Law Chips Away at Parental Rights,"
NewsMax.com, November 3, 2023, https://www.newsmax.com/michael
dorstewitz/california-newsom-parents/2023/11/03/id/1140888/.
10. Tyler Kingkade, "'We're Coming for Your Children' Chant at NYC Drag
March Elicits Outrage, but Activists Say It's Taken Out of Context,"
NBC News, June 27, 2023, https://www.nbcnews.com/nbc-out/nbc-out
-proud/re-coming-children-chant-nyc-drag-march-elicits-outrage-activists
-say-rcna91341.

CHAPTER 2: A LETTER OF LOST LOVE
1. Adapted from J. Allan Petersen, *The Myth of the Greener Grass* (Wheaton,
IL: Tyndale House, 1984), 200.
2. Associates for Biblical Research, "The Shiloh Excavations," accessed May 8,
2024, BibleArchaeology.org, https://biblearchaeology.org/research/new
-testament-era/3080-the-king-and-i-the-apostle-john-and-emperor-
domitian-part-1.
3. Michael Guillen, *Believing Is Seeing* (Carol Stream, IL: Tyndale Refresh,
2021), 66–71.

CHAPTER 3: A LETTER TO A SUFFERING CHURCH
1. Chike Uzuegbunam, "My College Tried to Stop Me from Speaking about
Religion. Now, We'll Meet in the Supreme Court," *Washington Post*,
January 11, 2021, https://www.washingtonpost.com/opinions/2021/01/11
/supreme-court-free-speech-georgia-gwinnett-college/.

2. K. J. Lynum, "Christian Students Receive $800k in Free Speech Lawsuit Ruling," Campus Reform, July 11, 2022, https://www.campusreform .org/article/christian-students-receive-800k-in-free-speech-lawsuit -ruling-/19821.
3. Uzuegbunam, "My College Tried to Stop Me from Speaking about Religion"; Lynum, "Christian Students Receive $800k in Free Speech Lawsuit Ruling."
4. David de Bruyn, "'Hate'—A Word Like 'Atheism,'" Religious Affections Ministries, April 21, 2020, https://religiousaffections.org/articles/articles -on-culture/hate-a-word-like-atheism/.
5. Frederick M. Hess and Jay P. Greene, "It's Time to Roll Back Campus DEI Bureaucracies," American Enterprise Institute, September 19, 2022, https://www.aei.org/op-eds/its-time-to-roll-back-campus-dei -bureaucracies/.
6. Ursula Westwood, "Domitian's Attitude to the Jews and Judaism," *Akroterion*, vol. 58, 2013, University of Stellenbosch, Department of Ancient Studies, https://go.gale.com/ps/i.do?p=AONE&u=anon ~26cb6263&id=GALE|A417473643&v=2.1&it=r&sid=googleScholar &asid=f0cd73fd.
7. John Piper, "Things Are Worse Than and Better Than They Seem," Desiring God, June 6, 1993, https://www.desiringgod.org/messages /things-are-worse-than-and-better-than-they-seem.

CHAPTER 4: A LETTER TO THE CHURCH NEAR SATAN'S THRONE
1. National Transportation Safety Board, "File No. 1-0016, Aircraft Accident Report, Eastern Air Lines, Inc., L-1011, N310EA, Miami, Florida, December 29, 1972," NTSB.gov, June 14, 1973, https://www.ntsb.gov /investigations/AccidentReports/Reports/AAR7314.pdf; CBS Miami, "50 Years Have Passed Since Eastern Airlines Flight 401 Crashed into the Everglades," CBS News, December 29, 2022, https://www.cbsnews .com/miami/news/50-years-have-passed-since-eastern-airlines-flight-401 -crashed-into-the-everglades/; Local 10, "Eastern Flight 401: A Survivor's Story," Local10.com, December 29, 2012, https://www.local10.com /news/2012/12/29/eastern-flight-401-a-survivors-story/.
2. Jake Emmett, "Just What Does Running a Marathon Do to Your Body?," MarathonHandbook.com, January 16, 2023, https://marathonhandbook .com/the-physiology-of-marathon-running/; Francis Chin, "When Fit People Get Heart Attacks," Bystander, September 2006, https://bystander .homestead.com/run_heart_attack.html.

3. Adam Gabbatt, "Losing Their Religion: Why US Churches Are on the Decline," *The Guardian*, January 22, 2023, https://www.theguardian .com/us-news/2023/jan/22/us-churches-closing-religion-covid -christianity.

CHAPTER 5: A LETTER TO THE CHURCH OF JEZEBEL

1. Frank Bergman, "WEF Calls for AI to Rewrite Bible, Create 'Religions That Are Actually Correct,'" Slay News, June 10, 2023, https://slaynews .com/news/wef-ai-rewrite-bible-create-religions-actually-correct/; Jacob Rosenberg, "AI May Soon Create 'Religions That Are Actually Correct' and 'Write a New Bible,' Says Famous Israeli Historian," All Israel News, September 13, 2023, https://allisrael.com/ai-may-soon-create-religions -that-are-actually-correct-and-write-a-new-bible-says-famous-israeli -historian.
2. TOI Staff, "Yuval Noah Harari Warns AI Can Create Religious Texts, May Inspire New Cults," *Times of Israel*, May 3, 2023, https://www .timesofisrael.com/yuval-noah-harari-warns-ai-can-create-religious -texts-may-inspire-new-cults/.
3. Bergman, "WEF Calls for AI to Rewrite Bible."
4. *Merriam-Webster*, s.v. "antinomian (*n.*)," accessed May 13, 2024, https://www.merriam-webster.com/dictionary/antinomian.

CHAPTER 6: A LETTER TO A DEAD CHURCH

1. Holcomb B. Noble and Douglas Martin, "John Kenneth Galbraith, 97, Dies; Economist Held a Mirror to Society," *New York Times*, April 30, 2006, https://www.nytimes.com/2006/04/30/obituaries/john-kenneth -galbraith-97-dies-economist-held-a-mirror-to.html. Dialogue is based on a narrative in the original source.
2. G. Michael Hopf, "Hard Times," GMichaelHopf.com, https://www .gmichaelhopf.com/hard-times. See also, Amanda van Eck Duymaer van Twist and Suzanne Newcombe, "Strauss–Howe Generational Theory," in James Crossley and Alastair Lockhart (eds.) *Critical Dictionary of Apocalyptic and Millenarian Movements*, January 15, 2021, https://www .cdamm.org/articles/strauss-howe.
3. Linda Feldmann, "Is Politics the New Religion?," *Christian Science Monitor*, May 12, 2021, https://www.csmonitor.com/USA/Politics /2021/0512/Is-politics-the-new-religion.
4. Craig S. Keener, *The NIV Application Commentary: Revelation* (Grand Rapids: Zondervan, 2000), 145.

CHAPTER 7: THE MOST JOYFUL LETTER

1. Charles Haddon Spurgeon, "A Call to the Lord's Own Flock," in C. H. Spurgeon, *Return, O Shulamite! and Other Sermons Preached in 1884* (New York: Robert Carter & Brothers, 1885), 378.

2. George W. Bush, "President Bush Discusses Defense Transformation at West Point, Eisenhower Hall, United States Military Academy, West Point, New York," GeorgeWBush-Whitehouse.Archives.gov, December 9, 2008, https://georgewbush-whitehouse.archives.gov/news /releases/2008/12/20081209-3.html.

3. NASA, Apollo 8 Flight Journal, "Day 1: The Green Team and Separation," last updated March 24, 2024, https://www.nasa.gov/history/afj/ap08fj /03day1_green_sep.html; NASA, Apollo 8 Flight Journal, "The Maroon Team," last updated December 29, 2004, https://web.archive.org/web /20080107002315/hrtps://history.nasa.gov/ap08fj/04day1_maroon.htm; Courtney G. Brooks, James M. Grimwood, and Loyd S. Swenson Jr., *Chariots for Apollo: A History of Manned Lunar Spacecraft* (Washington, DC: NASA, 1979), 277, https://www.nasa.gov/wp-content/uploads /2023/03/sp-4205.pdf.

4. American Public Media, "Earthrise: The Picture of Our Planet that Changed the World," *Brains On! Universe*, December 25, 2018, https:// www.brainson.org/episode/2018/12/25/earthrise-photo-solar-system.

5. "Apollo 8—Christmas Eve 1968," https://www.ittc.ku.edu/~evans /aviation/apollo8/.

CHAPTER 8: A LETTER TO A LUKEWARM CHURCH

1. Christy Heather, "10 Tragic Deaths That Rocked Extreme Sports," March 4, 2018, Listverse.com, https://listverse.com/2018/03/04/10 -tragic-deaths-that-rocked-extreme-sports/; Beth Hillyer, "Jimmy Hall's Final Adventure," Hawaii News Now, May 19, 2007, https://www .hawaiinewsnow.com/story/6539443/jimmy-halls-final-adventure/.

2. John MacArthur, *Because the Time Is Near: John MacArthur Explains the Book of Revelation* (Chicago: Moody, 2007), 99.

CHAPTER 9: RECLAIMING OUR TRUE IDENTITY IN CHRIST

1. Gregory Koukl and Alan Shlemon, "The 'Insider' Movement,'" Stand to Reason, November 1, 2012, https://www.str.org/w/the-insider-movement. Italics in the original.

About the Author

Dr. Michael Youssef is a pastor, bestselling author, and internationally respected Bible teacher. Born in Egypt, he lived in Lebanon and Australia before coming to the United States and fulfilling a childhood dream of becoming an American citizen. Dr. Youssef holds multiple degrees, including a PhD in cultural anthropology from Emory University. He founded The Church of The Apostles in Atlanta in 1987, and the church became the launching pad for *Leading The Way with Dr. Michael Youssef,* an international media ministry that now reaches audiences in nearly every major city in the world. His Middle Eastern heritage, keen understanding of Christian worldview issues, and unwavering passion for the gospel have given Dr. Youssef the unique ability to speak boldly into today's issues. He has authored more than fifty books, including popular titles *Heaven Awaits, Saving Christianity?, Life-Changing Prayers, Hope for This Present Crisis, Never Give Up,* and *Is the End Near?* He and his wife reside in Atlanta and have four grown children and fourteen grandchildren.

Connect with
Dr. Michael Youssef!

Follow Dr. Youssef for life-giving truth, behind-the-scenes ministry updates, and much more.

MichaelYoussef.com

 MichaelAYoussef

 Michael A. Youssef

CP2011

Biblical Encouragement for You—Anytime, Anywhere

Leading The Way with Dr. Michael Youssef is passionately proclaiming uncompromising Truth through every major form of media, empowering you to know and follow Christ. There are many FREE ways you can connect with Dr. Youssef's teachings:

- Thousands of sermons and articles online
- TV and radio programs worldwide
- Apps for your phone or tablet
- A monthly magazine, and more!

Learn more at **LTW.org/Connect**